PORTO

Travel with Marco Polo Insider Tips

INSIDER TIP Your shortcut to a great experience

MARCO POLO TOP HIGHLIGHTS

TORRE DOS CLÉRIGOS 1
To get an overview of Porto, you can climb Portugal's tallest church tower and contemplate the city from above!

📷 *Tip: Use your camera's panorama function to capture the view – you can frame the whole of Porto!*

➤ p. 34

RIBEIRA 2
Narrow medieval alleyways crowd behind the colourful houses and boutique restaurants of the waterfront. It's the stuff of postcards.

➤ p. 40

SÉ DO PORTO 3
Porto's cathedral reveals 900 years of architectural history: from Romanesque to Gothic, and from Baroque through to the present.

➤ p. 38

PONTE DOM LUÍS I 4
Porto's double-decker bridge dates from 1886 and is surely the city's most famous landmark (photo).

📷 *Tip: To capture the iron bridge in all its glory against the colourful backdrop of the Ribeira, take your photo from the Mosteiro da Serra do Pilar.*

➤ p. 39

MERCADO DO BOLHÃO 5
The traditional market hall has been restored to its former glory after years of renovations.

📷 *Tip: For the best shot of the freshest fruit and fish, head down at 8am when the market opens.*

➤ p. 31 and p. 82

PALÁCIO DA BOLSA ★
A touch of the Alhambra pervades the extravagant Stock Exchange Palace. No holds were barred when this magnificent building was designed in the 19th century.

➤ p. 42

PORT CELLARS ★
Port, the region's liquid gold, rests in ancient barrels in the long, stone warehouses of Vila Nova de Gaia. Take a look, then try it for yourself!

➤ p. 53

ESTAÇÃO DE SÃO BENTO ★
Not your everyday station concourse: 20,000 tiles tell stories in blue and white as the trains disappear into tunnels beneath the hilly city.

➤ p. 33

PARQUE DE SERRALVES ★
A sensational world of culture with stunning architecture and exciting contemporary art.
📷 *Tip: Take time to explore the magnificent park – you'll find countless works of art to photograph between the trees.*

➤ p. 55

JARDINS DO PALÁCIO DE CRISTAL ★
A romantic garden oasis with plenty of culture and dreamy views over the river.
📷 *Tip: Take a stroll to the far end of the park; the turrets are the ideal spot for a panoramic shot.*

➤ p. 45

CONTENTS

⏲	Plan your visit	🍴	Eating/drinking	☂	Rainy day activities
€-€€€	Price categories	🛍	Shopping	🐖	Budget activities
(*)	Premium-rate phone number	🍸	Going out	👶	Family activities
		🌴	Top beaches	⚑	Classic experiences

(📖 A2) Refers to the removable pull-out map
(📖 a2) Refers to the inset street maps on the pull-out map
(0) Located off the map

CONTENTS

MARCO POLO TOP HIGHLIGHTS
2 Top ten highlights

BEST OF PORTO
10 ... when it rains
11 ...on a budget
12 ... with children
13 ... classic experiences

GET TO KNOW PORTO
16 Discover Porto
19 At a glance
20 Understand Porto
23 True or false?

26 SIGHTSEEING
30 Baixa
37 Old Town
44 Porto West
48 Foz do Douro
52 Vila Nova de Gaia
55 Other sights
57 Around Porto

60 EATING & DRINKING

74 SHOPPING

86 NIGHTLIFE

ACTIVE & RELAXED
98 Sport & wellness
100 Festivals & events
102 Sleep well

DISCOVERY TOURS
108 Porto at a glance
111 Matosinhos by bike
114 Porto's lesser-known east side
116 Porto's street art

GOOD TO KNOW
120 **CITY BREAK BASICS**
Arrival, Getting around, Emergencies, Essentials, Weather
128 **PORTUGUESE WORDS & PHRASES**
Don't be lost for words
130 **HOLIDAY VIBES**
Books, films, music & blogs
132 **TRAVEL PURSUIT**
The Marco Polo holiday quiz
134 **INDEX & CREDITS**
136 **DOS AND DON'TS**
How to avoid slip-ups & blunders

The Casa da Música boasts postmodern architecture and excellent acoustics

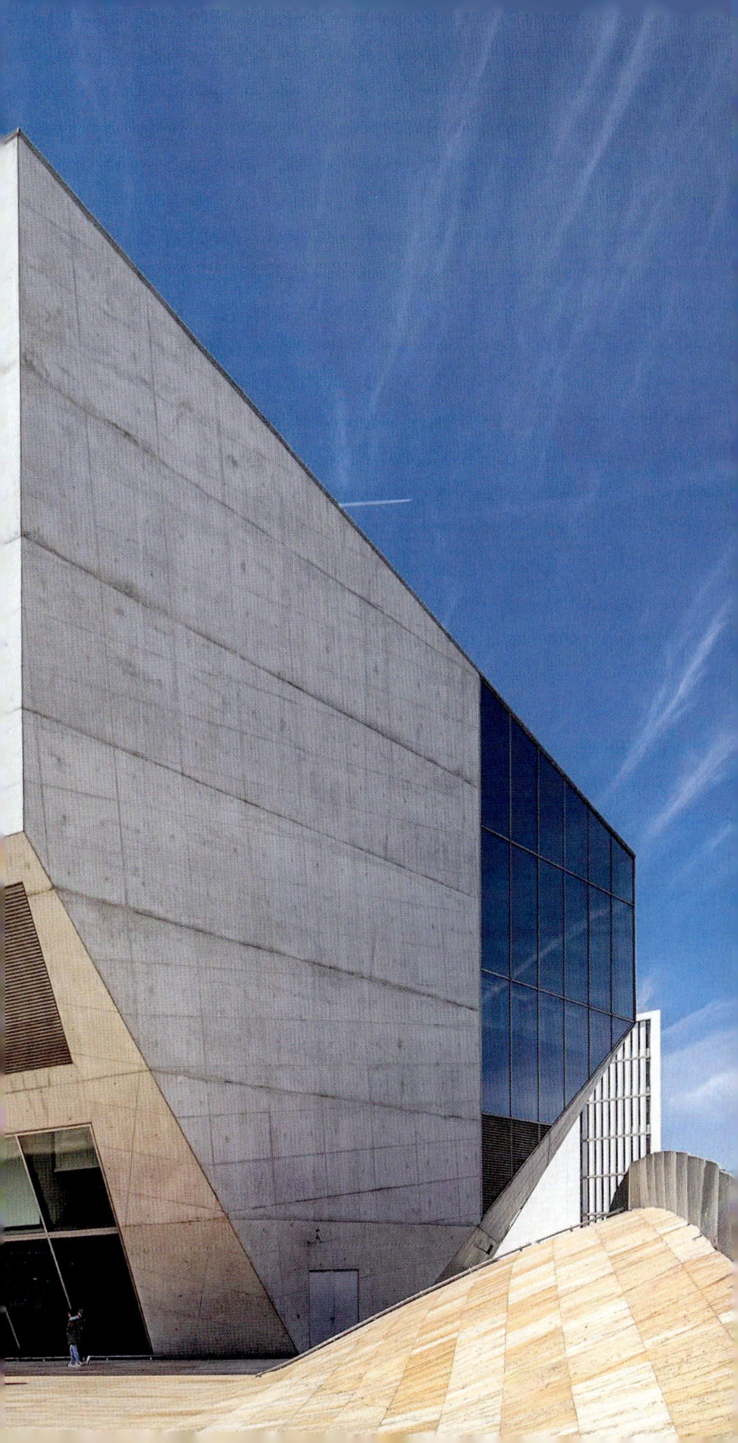

BEST OF PORTO

Blue and white tiles everywhere you look – even in the cloisters of the cathedral

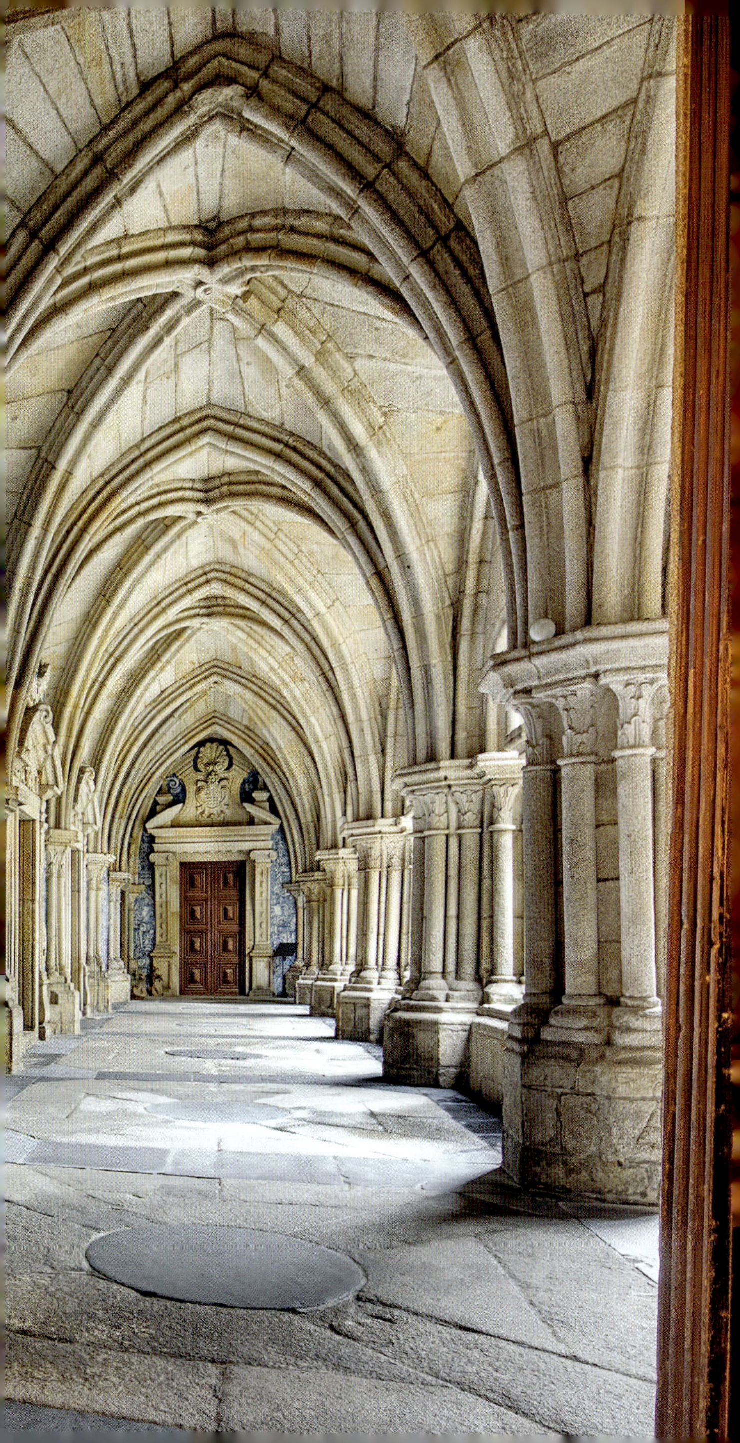

BEST WHEN IT RAINS

ACTIVITIES TO BRIGHTEN YOUR DAY

BROWSE LIKE JK ROWLING
We promise it's worth the queue! Once you've marvelled at the *Livraria Lello*'s magnificent staircase, grab a good book and find a place to read in the café next door. It's not hard to imagine the Harry Potter author doing something similar!
➤ p. 34, Sightseeing, p. 78, Shopping

FOR THE SAKE OF ART
The *Museu Nacional de Soares dos Reis* exhibits Portuguese paintings from the 19th and 20th centuries alongside priceless musical instruments, furniture, jewellery and porcelain.
➤ p. 37, Sightseeing

MONEY, MONEY, MONEY
The sheer splendour of the imposing *Palácio da Bolsa* is enough to make you forget the rain. And why not stay for lunch and mingle with the financial crowd in the *O Comercial* restaurant?
➤ p. 42, Sightseeing

ARCHITECTURE & MUSIC
While away a rainy afternoon in the futuristic *Casa da Música* (photo). Start with a guided tour behind the scenes of this phenomenal concert hall, then stop off at the café or restaurant before enjoying an evening concert in the *Sala Suggia*.
➤ p. 47, Sightseeing, p. 94, Nightlife

ADMIRE THE FISH
If it's raining, head inside and admire the many sea creatures at *Sea Life*: the aquarium's 31 tanks are home to some 3,000 creatures! The penguins are particularly cool.
➤ p. 51, Sightseeing

BEST ON A BUDGET

FOR SMALLER WALLETS

FABULOUS PHOTOS IN THE OLD PRISON
The *Centro Português de Fotografia* is not to be missed. The historic prison building alone is well worth a visit; the labyrinthine halls and cells display a fascinating range of photographs and old cameras. What's more, you can visit the whole thing free of charge!
➤ p. 33, Sightseeing

A BANK FOR FREE
No, you can't sort your finances here! The *Banco de Materiais* is a municipal archive for decorative home furnishings. It costs nothing to enjoy the beautiful *azulejo* tilework, stucco, iron struts and doorknobs.
➤ p. 36, Sightseeing

MUSEUMS FOR LESS
A combo ticket opens the doors to all the different branches of the city's *Museu do Porto* for just 8 euros. The *Museu do Vinho do Porto* and the *Casa do Infante* are particularly worth a visit.
➤ p. 41, Sightseeing

FLORA FOR FREE
It's hard to believe, but it's free to enjoy the beautifully kept *Jardim Botânico*! The *Galeria da Biodiversidade*, in the garden's main building, is well worth visiting too – luckily, it's also free every second Sunday of the month between 10am and 1pm.
➤ p. 46, Sightseeing

ALL SORTS OF DISCOUNTS
If you're planning on doing a lot of sightseeing, the *Porto Card* is for you. It offers free travel on the metro (photo) and city buses, free museum visits and all sorts of other discounts.
➤ p. 126, Good to know

11

BEST WITH CHILDREN

FUN FOR YOUNG & OLD

VOYAGE OF DISCOVERY
The *World of Discoveries* offers a playful insight into the golden age of Portuguese seafaring – you'll even be treated to a boat trip to India (photo)!
➤ p. 43, Sightseeing

TRAMWAY NOSTALGIA
Share your budding engineer's enthusiasm with these fascinating old trams, some of which would have been pulled by horses! The *Museu do Carro Eléctrico* will transport you back in time through the history of trams in Porto.
➤ p. 46, Sightseeing

A PLAYGROUND BY THE SEA
Let your little ones loose at this wooden playground above the *Praia do Homem do Leme*, in Foz do Douro. The marine setting is perfect for playing pirates, with ropes galore for swinging and shinning up.
➤ p. 50, Sightseeing

PORTUGAL'S BIGGEST URBAN PARK
Young and old alike can let off steam at the *Parque da Cidade* in Matosinhos. Kick a ball around the spacious parkland or cycle through the vast swathes of forest. And if you still have the energy, visit the *Pavilhão da Água*, a fun science museum all about water and hydropower.
➤ p. 51, Sightseeing

5D VIEW OF PORTO
So the kids are getting tired of walking (to be fair, they're not the only ones), but you're not quite ready to call it a day. Why not embark on this interactive journey at the 5D cinema *Look at Porto*, in Vila Nova de Gaia?
➤ p. 55, Sightseeing

BEST 🚩
CLASSIC EXPERIENCES

ONLY IN PORTO

TALES IN TILES
Porto is the city of granite … and also of *azulejos* (photo). The famous tiles adorn many of the churches and even the spectacular railway station. You can see them for yourself and discover their history at the *Estação de São Bento*.
➤ p. 33, Sightseeing

PORTO FROM ABOVE
If you're short on time but still want to see the whole city, why not climb the 76m-high *Torre dos Clérigos*? Portugal's highest church tower is a truly fantastic landmark, and the city of Porto will be at your feet.
➤ p. 34, Sightseeing

IN SEARCH OF PORT
Porto is famous for its port wine, even though the grapes themselves grow far upstream in the Douro Valley and the wineries are located in Vila Nova de Gaia. The *Museu do Vinho do Porto* explains Porto's role in the port wine business – and, afterwards, it would be rude not to taste a glass at the excellent bar.
➤ p. 41, Sightseeing

MUNCH ON … TRIPE?
Granted, *tripas* might not be everyone's cup of tea. But the people of Porto love it, and you might find yourself converted when it's cooked with spicy white beans – e.g. at *Tasca da Badalhoca*.
➤ p. 71, Eating & drinking

SIGHTSEE FROM THE WATER
The *Cruzeiro das 6 Pontes* is the perfect introduction to Porto's photogenic waterfront. As well as the six bridges and the port cellars, you'll even catch a glimpse of the sea on this boat trip that lasts just under an hour!
➤ p. 110, Discovery tours

13

GET TO KNOW PORTO

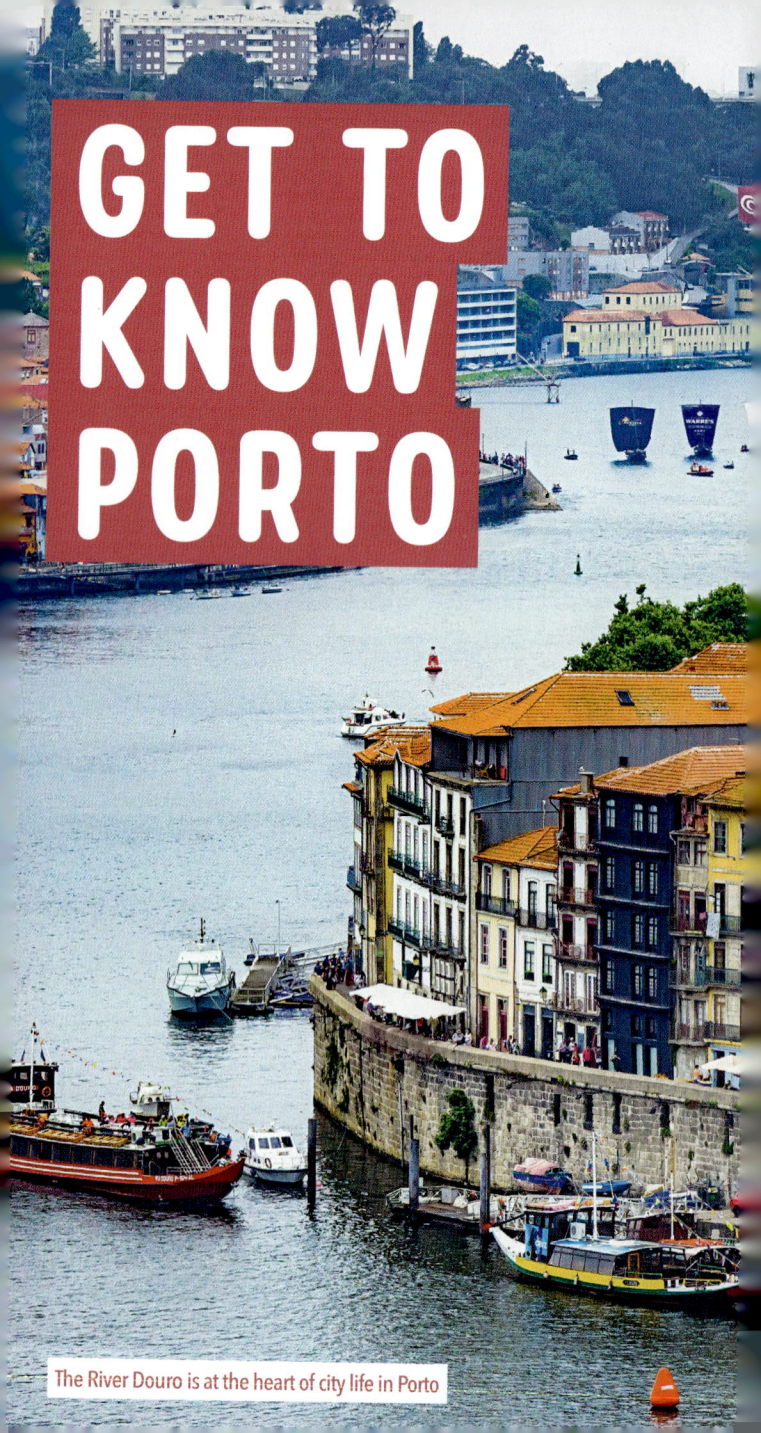

The River Douro is at the heart of city life in Porto

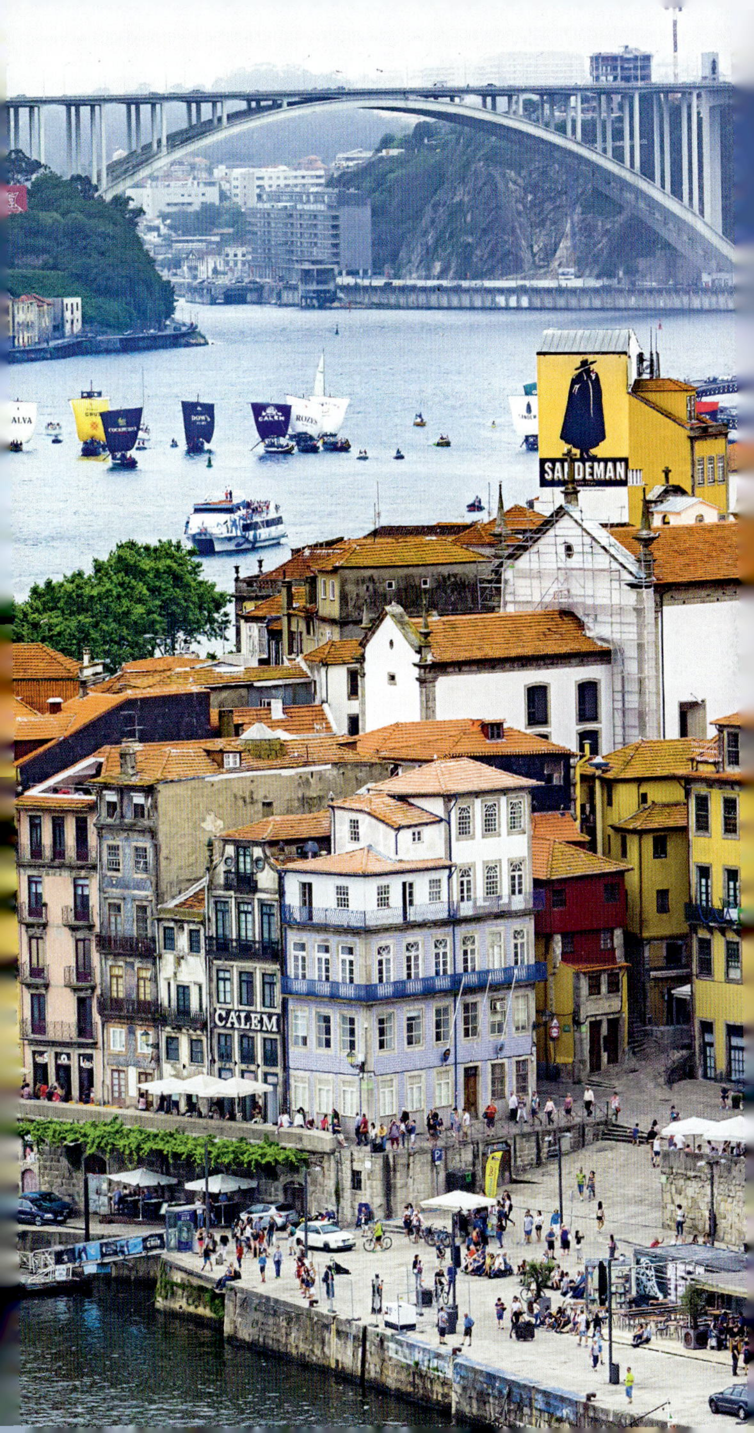
SANDEMAN
ALVA
DOW'S
CALEM
ROZES
CALEM

DISCOVER PORTO

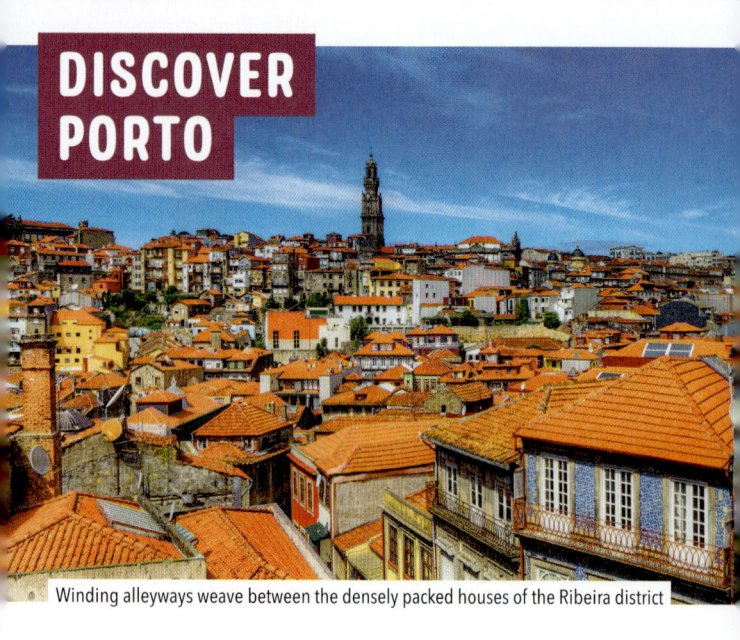

Winding alleyways weave between the densely packed houses of the Ribeira district

Porto really is the stuff of poetry: a city of granite adorned with gleaming walls of tiles; a place brimming with romance and more than its fair share of breathtaking views, thanks to the steep, rocky banks of the River Douro. Besides, the ups and downs of this undulating city only serve to sweeten the taste of the port – many a gloomy day has been brightened by a tour of a port cellar!

CHARM MEETS CULTURE

Yes, it's true, Portugal's north is a lot wetter and chillier than its sunny south. But even in the winter months you'll often find yourself basking under sunshine and blue skies, when Porto is truly dreamy. And the summer months are much drier, in any case. In the last decade, Portugal's second city has emerged from relative

---

2nd century BCE–5th century CE
Roman rule

8th–12th century CE
Moorish invasions of the Iberian Peninsula

From 1415
Porto benefits from Portugal's rise as a maritime and colonial power

1580–1640
Spanish rule of Portugal

1809
Collapse of the Ponte das Barcas over the Douro

1832
Liberal king Dom Pedro IV defeats his absolutist brother Miguel with the help of the people of Porto

GET TO KNOW PORTO

obscurity, at least from a tourism perspective, to rival Lisbon; indeed, many visitors declare Porto to be the more beautiful of the two cities (a fact that is staunchly refuted by Lisboetas). Porto has certainly blossomed in recent years, with tourism playing its part in this transformation. No longer shabby and grey, today this bustling city on the Douro is bright and charming with an incredible cultural programme of concerts and (folk) festivals, which the locals enjoy just as much as the visitors.

THE RIVER MEETS THE SEA
You'll quickly get a feel for the city, especially if you take a boat trip on the Douro to admire the picture-book scenery. Colourful Ribeira houses adorn one side of the river, while port cellars are on the other; you can even catch a glimpse of the sea, as Porto (unlike Lisbon!) sits right on the Atlantic Ocean – and even has beautiful sandy beaches!

WHEN IN PORTO … WORK?
Stay for a few days and you might find time to delve deeper and venture beyond the UNESCO-protected historic centre and picture-perfect scenery. What drives the people of Porto (apart from FC Porto's position in the league table, of course!)? What makes the city so special beside the tourist hotspots? The Portuguese have a saying for their most important cities: *Braga reza, Coimbra estuda, Porto trabalha e Lisboa diverte-se* (when in Braga, pray; when in Coimbra, study; when in Porto, work; and when in Lisbon, have fun). Although evidently

1910 Portugal's king is overthrown and the republic is declared

1933 Dictatorship established under António de Oliveira Salazar

1974 The Carnation Revolution ends the dictatorship

1986 Portugal joins the EU

From 2015 Boom in tourism triples the number of overnight stays in five years

2022-25 Construction of the new Linha Rosa metro line sees building sites mushroom in the west of the city centre

stereotyped, there is certainly a grain of truth in the saying, and Porto is still very much the city of graft, with many medium-sized businesses in the city itself and of course the port of Leixões, one of the most important in the country. Some say that "Lisbon spends the money earned in Porto". In fact, that has been the case since the days when Portugal was ruled by kings and queens. The ruling class in the capital lived a life of splendour, while the bourgeoisie, mainly enterprising port wine merchants, called the shots in Porto. This explains why Porto's palace, its most important building, is not a royal retreat, but the former Stock Exchange; to this day it remains the seat of the Chamber of Commerce.

THE TOURISM BOOM

Glittering gold leaf and glorious *azulejo* façades adorn Porto's many churches. However, not all that glitters is gold in Porto. The city's growing tourism industry, in particular, has incurred its fair share of displeasure among some of Porto's residents. This fallout stems not only from the hordes of tourists pushing their way through the alleyways of the cathedral district and the Ribeira or blocking the streets in hour-long queues at Livraria Lello in order to achieve the ultimate Instagram shot. The locals have learned to stay well away from these hotspots. What really grinds people's gears are the skyrocketing property prices: in the rush to provide holiday lets, city-centre residents are being forced out of their homes and into the surrounding areas as house prices rise disproportionately. Young families don't stand a chance and plenty a neighbourhood is in danger of losing its ambience to gentrification. It now falls to politicians to stop the situation from escalating further, not least to the mayor, Rui Moreira, an independent supported by the centre-right. Of course, Porto benefits greatly from tourism, but a path to growth needs to be found that doesn't exclude the locals.

ENJOY!

Porto is a pleasure, plain and simple, whether you're sipping on a glass of smooth port, savouring a *francesinha* with its spicy sauce or admiring the city's breathtaking views and thrilling architecture. And the great thing is that the people of Porto really enjoy their city too. Classical music enthusiasts will be enchanted by the Casa da Música, while rock fans will enjoy the first-class line-ups at the open-air festivals in summer. At the weekend, locals enjoy strolling along the banks of the Douro or the Atlantic, or visiting the city's free museums and many green oases. So why not join them? Take a seat on the romantic Passeio das Virtudes at sunset and gaze in wonder at the beauty of the golden Douro.

INSIDER TIP
After-work beers with a dreamy view

GET TO KNOW PORTO

AT A GLANCE

232,000
inhabitants in Porto city centre

1.8 million in the metropolitan area (Birmingham: 1.15 million)

19–22%
Alcohol content of port

Sherry: 15–22%
Vinho verde: 8.5–11.5%

7 RAINY DAYS
in July (17 in December)

London: 11 in July
(16 in December

PORTO'S BRIDGES ACROSS THE DOURO

6

Lisbon only has two bridges across the Tagus

AUGUST WATER TEMPERATURE IN THE ATLANTIC

19°

VINEYARDS IN THE PORTO AREA

0

Port grapes grow 100km upstream in the Douro Valley

LAYERS IN A FRANCESINHA

At least 9: 2 slices of toast, cooked ham, mortadella, escalope, 2 types of sausage, cheese, egg, spicy red sauce and chips

FC PORTO

Approx. 140,000 club members
(Manchester United: approx. 50,000 season ticket holders)

5,600 residents per km^2
Almost the same as London, which has 5,640

CHURCH TOWER WITH THE MOST STEPS: TORRE DOS CLÉRIGOS (240)

UNDERSTAND PORTO

SMOOTH WATERS

When the river meets the sea: where would Porto be without its water? The city owes almost everything to the Douro and the Atlantic; from its name (port, in case you hadn't guessed!) to its waterfront atmosphere (there isn't a view over the river that doesn't scream harbour romance!) and its economic success. The Douro was once used to transport the wine which was transformed into precious port in the cellars of Vila Nova de Gaia. Even today, the port of Leixões plays an important role in the country's economy and, let's face it, Porto wouldn't attract so many tourists if it were tucked away at the heart of the country's hinterland. And once you've toured the city and taken countless photos of the picturesque banks of the Douro, you can take a tram to the beach for an afternoon of relaxation. Where else can you enjoy such a perfect combination? Not in Lisbon, that's for sure.

ISLAND CONNECTIONS

Taylor, Graham, Cockburn, Croft … Why do so many ports have English names? The links with the UK go back a long way and are close-knit. Much closer than with Portugal's only direct neighbour, Spain, in fact. In 1386, England and Portugal signed the Treaty of Windsor. As early as 1387, the two nations then sealed the deal with the marriage of João I, the founder of the Aviz dynasty, and the English Princess Philippa of Lancaster in Porto Cathedral. Today, this is the oldest diplomatic alliance still in force in Europe.

By the mid-17th century, Portugal's economy, not least its agriculture, was so badly affected by 60 years of Spanish rule and the exhausting Restoration War that even food had to be imported. To simplify trade between England and Portugal, the two nations signed the Methuen Treaty in 1703. This document allowed the English to sell products like food and textiles to Portugal at preferential tariffs and without trade barriers. Conversely, Portuguese wine and port could be exported to England unhindered. Such favourable terms saw more and more wine merchants settling in Porto, with some of these families still producing and selling port to this day.

A good 100 years later, Portugal once again called on the English, this time enjoying their military support in the battles against Napoleon's French troops. It became a real thorn in Napoleon's side that the country continued to uphold economic relations with England, despite his Continental Blockade.

THE UNCONQUERED CITY

Since 1834, Porto has proudly borne the honorific title of *Cidade Invicta*, the Unconquered City. The city has carried this title, alongside a coat of arms featuring an invincible dragon, since it was bestowed by the queen Dona Maria II as a mark of her gratitude for Porto's enduringly successful support

GET TO KNOW PORTO

of her father Dom Pedro IV in the Liberal Wars that had plagued the country. In 1831 to 1832, supporters of the absolutist Dom Miguel I besieged the city, but the people of Porto remained steadfastly on the side of his liberal brother and refused to back down, ultimately helping Dom Pedro IV to victory. The latter expressed his gratitude in a rather more unusual way: he bequeathed Porto his heart, which has been kept in the Igreja de Lapa since his death.

These days, FC Porto likes to continue this mantel of invincibility, adopting the fire-breathing dragon as its club symbol and the old city coat of arms as its emblem. Of course, probably best not to mention it to the locals, but unlike Dom Pedro, the Estádio do Dragão, the "dragon stadium", does see the odd home defeat from time to time!

HIT THE HAMMER ... ON THE HEAD?

The night of 23-24 June, or the *noite de São João*, is a special one in Porto, and no one sleeps a wink! The fireworks at midnight over the Douro are the highlight, but people enjoy the fun all night long. And there is a rather unusual tool for celebrating the festival: a plastic hammer, which is used for rapping your friends, neighbours and of course family on the head so as to drive away dark thoughts. Interestingly enough, before the age of plastic, leeks were the instrument of choice, with some people carrying on the tradition to this day. To add to the pleasure, the whole city smells of sardines, which are grilled out on the street, and goat, the heraldic animal of the bearded patron saint. And it goes without saying that there is no shortage of beer, wine and music. The next

The river was vital to the transportation of port to and from the cellars of Vila Nova de Gaia

day, the whole city turns out to watch the beautiful historic port boats, the *barcos rabelo*, battle it out in a thrilling regatta.

GREY GRANITE & BRILLIANT BLUE TILES

If it weren't for the countless *azulejos* that adorn Porto's houses and churches, the granite cityscape would probably tend towards the gloomy thanks to the dark stone from the surrounding quarries. When it rains, nothing could be bleaker given that most of the city's buildings are made from the grey rock. Luckily, the Portuguese of the 15th and 16th centuries rediscovered the Moorish craft of *azulejos*. The name betrays the art form's Arabic origins: *al-zulij* means small, polished stone. Painting the frescoes in such humidity was hard work and the ceramic tiles were initially only found inside royal palaces and wealthy churches. Over time, however, the church realised that the blue and white wall decorations were the perfect visual Bible lesson.

Since the 19th century, *azulejos* have brightened the façades of many churches and private houses. And not only do they look beautiful; they also serve a practical purpose: just like bathroom tiles, the *azulejos* protect the buildings from moisture. These days, *azulejos* are everywhere: keep an eye out as you stroll through the city and you'll be amazed where you spot them, from metro stops and railway stations to retaining walls and advertising boards.

Bible study in pictures: *azulejos* decorate the façade of the Igreja do Carmo

GET TO KNOW PORTO

A WINE CITY WITHOUT VINEYARDS

Porto, the city of port! You'd be forgiven for picturing vineyards and rustic wineries, but the reality is quite different. The famous fortified wine actually has very little to do with Porto itself: the grapes are grown around 100km upstream in the UNESCO-protected Alto Douro wine-growing region. Traditionally, the port was then carried down the Douro in wooden boats; today it's transported in lorries. The port is then left to mature in old barrels on the shady southern bank of the Douro, in Vila Nova de Gaia. So where does Porto come into play then? Only once the bottles are ready and the wine merchants, who have always lived and worked in neighbouring Porto, spring into action. At least the port wine institute, which regulates and controls the cultivation, processing and trade of port and other wines from the Douro is based in Porto. There's something!

BUDDING ARCHITECTS

Long before the renowned Faculdade de Arquitectura da Universidade do Porto (FAUP) was founded in 1979, the so-called *Escola do Porto* was already creating quite the splash in architectural circles. Its founder, Professor Fernando Távora (1923–2005), had devoted his life and work to the social aspects of architecture as early as the mid-20th century. Several of his students, not least Pritzker Architecture Prize winners Álvaro Siza Vieira (born 1933) and Eduardo Souto de Moura (born 1952), would go on

TRUE OR FALSE?

EFFING & BLINDING

"Puta que pariu!" Many a person from the south of Portugal has been known to cringe nervously when a colleague from Porto suddenly starts swearing in a meeting, phrases leaving their mouth you'd otherwise only expect to hear from a teenager. Those who call Porto home love to swear, and little makes them watch their tongue. In fact, most aren't even aware of their linguistic slips: in Porto, these words are just another part of everyday life, used as friendly and even affectionate fillers without sounding at all vulgar to their ears.

TRIPE EATERS?

Over in Lisbon, the people of Porto are rather disparagingly called *tripeiros*, or "tripe eaters", because of their passion for offal – and, yes, people in Porto do indeed love to eat tripe. It is, in fact, a point of pride for the city. When Prince Henry the Navigator readied his fleet for the conquest of Ceuta on the banks of the Douro back in 1415, the people of Porto gave the shirts off their backs along with their very best meat. As a result, all they were left with was offal. An emotional Henry thanked the *tripeiros* for their selflessness, and to this day tripe is cooked to perfection here in Porto. Try it for yourself!

to create some of the most famous buildings in Porto, as well as other parts of Portugal and beyond, becoming some of the best-known names in the world of architecture. The work of architecture professor Luís Pedro Silva is also much admired; he was the brains behind the futuristic Matosinhos cruise terminal, which opened in 2015.

FOOTBALL FEVER

The Portuguese love their football. Fact. Whether it's the national team, Cristiano Ronaldo or 'just' the local five-a-side, the people of Portugal take the sport seriously. But when it comes to that passion for *your* club, things escalate to a whole new level. Walk through the neighbourhoods of the Old Town and you'll be sure to see the blue and white flags of FC Porto waving from many a window. The club is ingrained in the city's DNA and the locals aren't willing to cede an inch to fans of Benfica Lisbon (a rare but not unheard-of breed here).

The *Futebol Clube do Porto* was founded in 1893, interestingly enough by a wine merchant who had discovered the ball game while travelling in England. It didn't take long for a good footballing rivalry to get underway with Lisbon, one which has continued throughout both clubs' histories to the present day. When the first nationwide championship was held in 1934/35, Porto was the first to claim the title, with dozens more to follow. FC Porto has also won the Champions League twice, in 1987 and 2004, and the city has rarely known celebrations like it. Jorge Nuno Pinto da Costa, born in Porto in 1937, was president of the club for a whopping 42 years (1982–2024), making him in many eyes the most successful club president in the history of sport.

The home of FC Porto is the Estádio do Dragão, which was built for the 2004 European Championships and is now one of the three largest stadiums in the country. Also in Porto is the Estádio do Bessa, another First Division stadium. This is the home of Boavista, which was founded in 1903 but has only won the Portuguese title once (back in 2001). Still, even the big clubs rarely enjoy an easy game against Boavista. The local matches against FC Porto are, of course, particularly exciting!

THE CITY'S FASTEST WOMAN

Rosa Mota – *a nossa Rosinha* ("our darling Rosa") – was born in Porto in 1958 and, now in her 60s, is almost as fast and wiry as ever. While the highlight of her sporting career was winning Olympic gold in the Seoul marathon in 1988, you'll still find her running in competitions and hitting times many 20-year-old amateur runners could only dream of. But what makes Rosa Mota so likeable is her down-to-earth character and the fact she never seems to tire of motivating the Portuguese to get exercising. She doesn't claim that everyone is a natural-born athlete, but simply promotes the many and diverse benefits of doing whatever exercise works for you. As a tribute to her career, the sports arena in Porto's Jardins do Palácio de Cristal was

GET TO KNOW PORTO

named after her in 1991. Rather ironically, the building and the name has since been taken over by a large beer manufacturer. Despite this, everyone in Porto still knows it as the Pavilhão Rosa Mota.

A BAROQUE GOLD RUSH

Warning! Gold overload! During the reign of absolutist King João V in the 18th century, the Igreja de Santa Clara and above all the Igreja de São Francisco were stuffed to the brim with gold after the Portuguese discovered the precious metal in Brazil. While the churches are actually Gothic, their interiors were adorned with priceless wood carvings decorated with gold leaf, known as *talha dourada*. You can see this incredible golden wood in many of the Portuguese churches that were embellished during the Baroque period, but none rival the magnificent Franciscan church in Porto.

Portugal's Baroque period saw a construction boom in Porto, largely driven by the Italian architect Nicolau Nasoni (1691–1773) who travelled to northern Portugal in 1725 and quickly made a name for himself as a talented architect, artist and master of interior design. He began by updating the cathedral in the Baroque style, redesigning the chancel and painting frescoes, before creating the loggia on the north side and the episcopal palace. He went on to adorn the Misericórdia and the Carmo churches with their Rococo façades, but his largest and most emblematic project (which took over 40 years, from 1731 to 1773!) was the construction of the Igreja dos Clérigos. Today, the church still bears the highest church tower in Portugal, a point of reference that can be seen from afar.

A whopping 300 kg of gold leaf adorns the Igreja de São Francisco

SIGHT SEEING

Before you start exploring Porto, head to Portugal's tallest church tower for a bird's eye view of the entire city. Next, take a boat trip along the Douro to see all six bridges, as well as most of the highlights along the hilly banks of Porto and Vila Nova de Gaia.

After just half a day you will have grasped a pretty good first impression of Porto. But you'll need a long weekend to really immerse yourself in Portugal's second-largest city. That should give you enough time to stroll down the many alleyways and to walk up

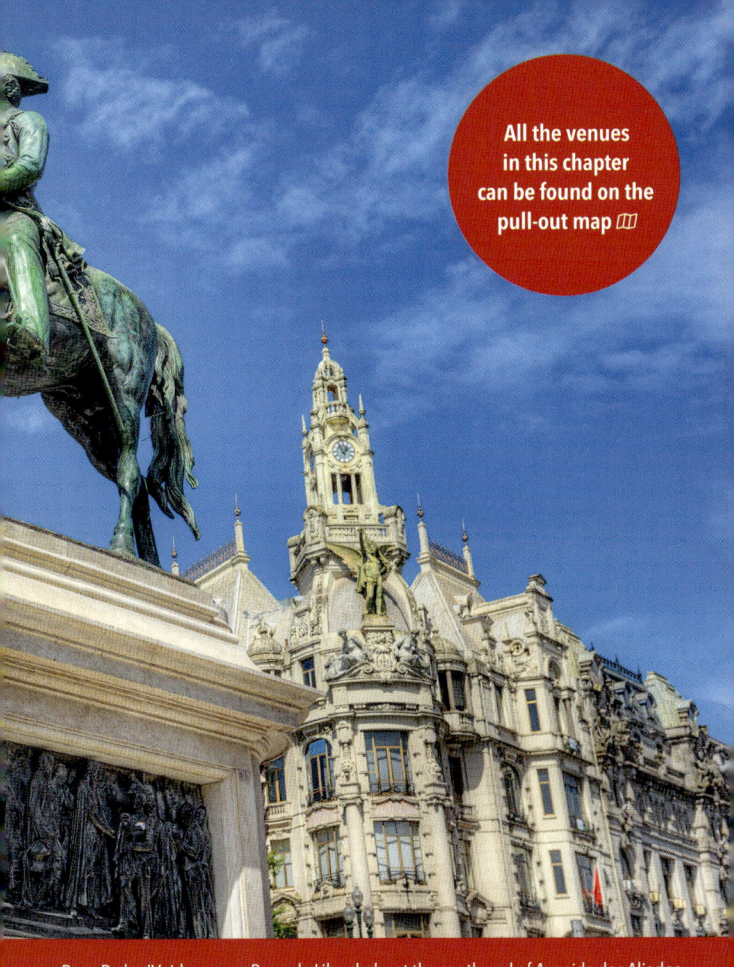

> **All the venues in this chapter can be found on the pull-out map**

Dom Pedro IV rides across Praça da Liberdade, at the south end of Avenida dos Aliados

and down the steps of the Old Town and the cathedral hill; you should also explore the sprawling Baixa with its squares, shopping streets and bars galore; and find time to wonder at the modern art and magnificent park of Serralves.

You can't possibly miss a trip to one of the port wine cellars in Vila Nova de Gaia; and you'd kick yourself if you didn't visit the upmarket neighbourhood of Foz do Douro – where you can rent a bike, hop on a historic tram or catch a bus to the shores of the Atlantic.

NEIGHBOURHOOD OVERVIEW

FOZ DO DOURO p. 48
Affluent estuary district with Atlantic beaches and plenty of joggers

PORTO WEST p. 44
Things get romantic in Massarelos, modern in Boavista and studious in Arrábida

VILA NOVA DE GAIA p. 52
Beyond Porto, but full of port!

MARCO POLO HIGHLIGHTS

★ AVENIDA DOS ALIADOS
A magnificent boulevard and the beating heart of the city – especially when there's a fiesta ➤ p. 30

★ ESTAÇÃO DE SÃO BENTO
Not bad for a station concourse: 20,000 blue-and-white tiles tell stories while the trains disappear into railway tunnels ➤ p. 33

★ TORRE DOS CLÉRIGOS
Portugal's highest church tower reveals a view of the entire city ➤ p. 34

★ SÉ DO PORTO
All of Porto's stylistic epochs in one space, from Romanesque to Gothic and from Baroque to the present ➤ p. 38

★ PONTE DOM LUÍS I
The double-decker iron bridge spans the Douro, and stars in all the best photos of Porto ➤ p. 39

★ RIBEIRA
Picturesque alleyways and colourful homes nestle in the smallest of spaces between river and rock face ➤ p. 40

★ PALÁCIO DA BOLSA
The height of opulence: the Chamber of Commerce pulled out all the stops with this lavish 19th-century palace ➤ p. 42

★ JARDINS DO PALÁCIO DE CRISTAL
Porto's gloriously romantic botanical garden is an oasis dotted with sculptures and fountains and with breathtaking views over the river ➤ p. 45

★ PORT CELLARS
Take a tour and uncover the secrets of port, then delight in tasting it for yourself – *Saúde*! ➤ p. 53

★ PARQUE DE SERRALVES
Enjoy the exciting exhibitions of contemporary art in the museum before venturing outside to discover more art and architecture in the vast park ➤ p. 55

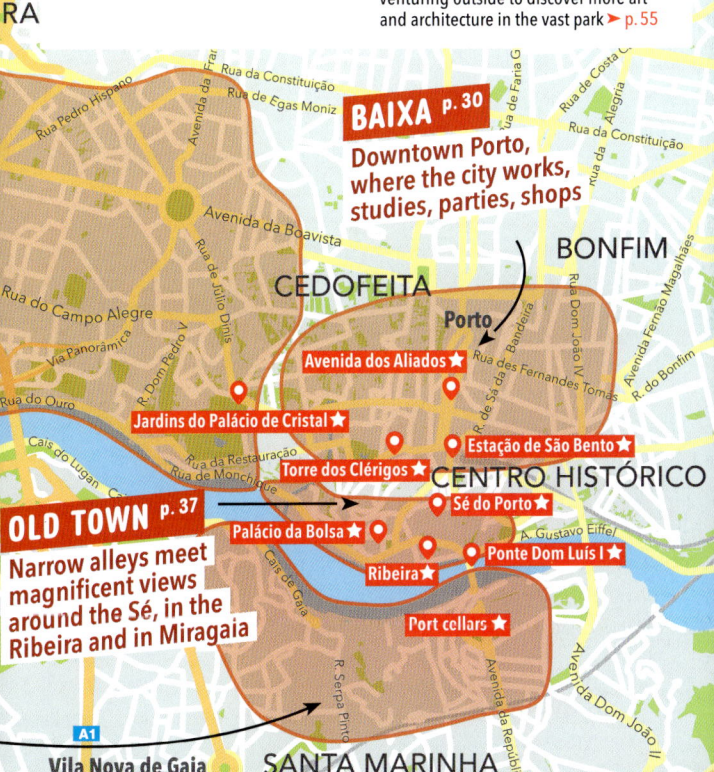

BAIXA p. 30
Downtown Porto, where the city works, studies, parties, shops

OLD TOWN p. 37
Narrow alleys meet magnificent views around the Sé, in the Ribeira and in Miragaia

BAIXA

Although Baixa translates roughly as "downtown", this city-centre district is set much higher up in the hills of Porto than, for example, the Ribeira district down on the riverbank.

But in every other sense, the Baixa is "Downtown Porto". This is where you'll find all the most important squares and shopping streets, the lively artists' quarter of Cedofeita, the university and the best bars, all the most famous attractions and a plethora of places to stay and eat. This is where the action is, both day and night.

While the boom in tourism has left a permanent mark on the streets of the Baixa, displacing more than a few residents, many can and do still live here. From west to east, the Baixa stretches downhill from the university district to Avenida dos Aliados and then back up again towards Praça da Batalha. In spite of the ups and downs, you can get around on foot here; in reality, there are no seriously long distances in the city centre.

WHERE TO START?

The magnificent **Avenida dos Aliados** *(□□ j6)* is the beating heart of the Baixa and the ideal starting point for exploring not only the Baixa, but also the cathedral district and the Ribeira. Take the metro (yellow line D) to get there. If you are driving, head for the Parque de Estacionamento Trindade (car park) just metres behind the city hall. Luckily, the city has a great bus service; from Carmo, especially, you can easily travel west to the Jardins do Palácio de Cristal, Serralves and Foz do Douro.

1 AVENIDA DOS ALIADOS ★

Here we are: the beating heart of Porto. This 250m-long boulevard connects the Praça da Liberdade and Porto's *Câmara Municipal* (at least, it will once the construction work on the new metro line is finished), forming a main artery through Porto. Whether the city is celebrating FC Porto's championship success, receiving a papal Mass, enjoying a summer concert, holding a demonstration or a parade or even New Year's Eve fireworks, life is always moving here. And it is a beautiful avenue – even if it didn't turn out to be quite as long as English architect Barry Parker had originally planned. In 1916, his intention was to create a 1km-long axis in honour of the Allied forces of World War I. Well, at least the name made it!

The Neoclassical *Câmara Municipal (Mon–Fri 9am–5pm)*, Porto's city hall at the northern end of the avenue, took its inspiration from the Flemish and northern French. Here, too, the tower was supposed to stand taller than its actual 70m (but construction had dragged on from 1920 to 1957). Its elegant entrance hall reveals an impressive black marble staircase and often hosts exhibitions. Elsewhere,

SIGHTSEEING

Eat your Big Mac surrounded by chandeliers and stained glass on the Avenida dos Aliados

the chic city banks boast neo-Baroque granite façades and striking foyers. Even *McDonald's* sticks to the theme:

INSIDER TIP
Big Mac in style

with crystal chandeliers hung high above the grease-smeared tables, it is certainly the most beautiful in the country, and the stained-glass windows are a reminder of the Café Imperial, which used to occupy the elegant building. Head diagonally opposite for another historic café: the tropical *Café Guarany* (see p. 64) has delighted local bankers and other guests since 1933.

Here, at the lower end of Avenida dos Aliados, you'll find two sculptures by Henrique Moreira: *Abundância*, which shows three naked boys in a reproach to affluent society; and the naked bronze *Juventude*, a flirtatious homage to youth. At the southern end of the magnificent avenue, meanwhile, a bronze *equestrian statue* of King Dom Pedro IV dominates the *Praça da Liberdade*. The 19th-century king won his fight for a liberal constitution against his absolutist brother Miguel, thanks to the help of the people of Porto. 📖 *j6*

2 MERCADO DO BOLHÃO ★

Following renovations between 2018 to 2022, this two-storey market hall is once again as good as new. A city market has been held here since the mid-19th century, but there had long been trouble with the unstable ground. A building was erected in 1914 with a Neoclassical façade and covered internal galleries, but business ground to a halt when the foundations subsided and the structure was in danger of collapsing. Now, at last, the people of Porto (and visitors, of course) can once again enjoy their

31

BAIXA

Mercado do Bolhão with all its fruit, vegetables, flowers, spices, fish and meat as well as all kinds of Portuguese specialities. The market also hosts an array of interesting events. *Mon–Fri 8am–8pm, Sat 8am–6pm, restaurants until midnight | Rua Formosa | mercadobolhao.pt | metro Bolhão | j5–6*

3 PRAÇA DA BATALHA

The name, "battle square", betrays its military history: bloody skirmishes between Christians and Moors are said to have taken place on the site, way back in the 10th century. Today, a number of intriguing buildings line the elongated *praça*. The first to catch the eye is the 18th-century Baroque *Igreja de Santo Ildefonso (Mon 3–5pm, Tue–Fri 9am–noon, 3–5pm, Sat 9am–1pm, 3–7pm, Sun 9–10am | 1 euro).* The church bears the work of tile artist Jorge Colaço: the piece from 1932 tells stories from the life of the Archbishop of Toledo in some 11,000 tiles.

On the southern side of the square is the *Teatro Nacional São João (guided tours Tue–Sat 12.30pm | 6 euros | tnsj.pt).* However, this rather eclectic building is only about 100 years old – the previous one from 1798 burnt down in 1908. Work started in the 1990s to restore the theatre to its former glory – after it had functioned as a cinema for years. Speaking of cinema, the Praça da Batalha was once a hotspot for evening entertainment, when the *Cine-Teatro Batalha* opened back in 1947 with space for some 900 visitors. Thankfully, the building, which boasts

SIGHTSEEING

a magnificent Art Deco façade, was given a new lease of life in 2022 as the *Batalha Centro de Cinema*. Another Art Deco cinema just next door, the Águia d'Ouro, was converted into the Hotel Moov Porto Centro. *Buses and trams Batalha | j6*

4 ESTAÇÃO DE SÃO BENTO ★ ▶

If it weren't for the trains departing from just behind the impressive entrance hall, you would be forgiven for mistaking this station for a palace. Incidentally, the trains disappear directly into the mountain: extensive tunnel work was needed at the end of the 19th century to build a connection from Campanhã station, 2.7km away. When the first steam train arrived at the former site of the São Bento de Ave Maria convent in 1896, only wooden shacks would have stood on either side of the tracks, instead of the grand station we know today.

Today's spectacular station concourse was inaugurated in 1916. Its 20,000 *azulejos*, carefully painted by tile artist Jorge Colaço, have certainly helped it onto the list of the most beautiful stations in the world. The 550m² space is divided into sections, with scenes from agriculture, viticulture and transport adorning the upper area. Further down, the tiles give a blue-and-white history lesson, including the story of Prince Henry the Navigator conquering Ceuta in 1415. So you need not worry if your train is delayed (a rare occurrence in Portugal, anyway), there's plenty to look at here! *Praça de Almeida Garrett | metro São Bento | j6*

5 RUA DAS FLORES

This charming pedestrianised street connects the Baixa with the areas along the riverbank. The street slopes gently downhill, lined with pretty façades, brightly painted electricity boxes, hip cafés and trendy shops. The "street of flowers" dates back to the early 16th century and was built under the patronage of King Manuel I at a time when the monasteries located here were still surrounded by fields and flower meadows. With the influx of noblemen and silversmiths, the shopping street, which was paved from 1542, became a distinctly wealthy neighbourhood. Dotted here and there you can still see the odd façade decorated with a noble coat of arms and a few long-established jewellers have also survived. The somewhat lamentable fact that most of the flowers on the wrought-iron balcony railings are plastic happily fails to detract from what is arguably the city's most beautiful street. *Metro São Bento | h-j 6-7*

6 CENTRO PORTUGUÊS DE FOTOGRAFIA ▶

This vast and slightly formidable 18th-century court and prison building held prisoners right up until the 1970s. The old prison cells and halls, the winding staircases and all the iron bars make for an impressive, if somewhat spine-chilling atmosphere. The Portuguese Centre of Photography moved into the old fortress-like building in 1997 following renovations. Today, the photo exhibitions change regularly, with a valuable collection of

BAIXA

old cameras and historical equipment also on display. *Tue–Fri 10am–6pm, Sat/Sun 3–7pm | free admission | Largo Amor de Perdição | cpf.pt | buses Cordoaria | ⏱ 30 mins | 📖 h6*

7 IGREJA & TORRE DOS CLÉRIGOS

Now this definitely is a landmark! The 76m-high granite tower is well worth the steep climb up 240 narrow steps, for you will be rewarded with a stunning view over the whole city. Perhaps unsurprisingly, the ⭐ 🚩 *Torre dos Clérigos* is Portugal's tallest church tower. Despite its stature, the structure has an almost delicate appearance. It was the masterpiece of Baroque Italian architect Nicolau Nasoni, who dedicated more than 30 years of his life to the church and its tower. Despite leaving his mark all over Porto, it is this work that remains his most famous. It seems appropriate that he should be buried in the crypt, just behind the lavish altar room. Upon completion, the tower quickly became a point of orientation for incoming ships as well as a clock tower for the people of Porto. In later years, it even became a telegraph station. Visit at noon when the Baroque organs of this colourful oval church are played in a short 🐷 lunchtime concert – free classical music! *Daily 9am–7pm | tower 8 euros, church is free | Rua São Filipe de Nery | torredosclerigos.pt | tram 22: Clérigos | ⏱ 1 hr (tower and church) | 📖 h6*

> **INSIDER TIP**
> Lunchtime organ concerts

8 LIVRARIA LELLO ⭐ 🚩

So what's the deal here? Despite needing to book a ticket online in advance, you will still find yourself queuing for at least ten minutes for an allocated time slot at this Art Nouveau bookshop, which opened in 1906. The shop owes its fame largely to the writer JK Rowling, who many claim drew inspiration here for her Harry Potter series. The building's bright neo-Gothic façade is of course eye-catching, but it is the interior – in particular the richly decorated, sweeping wooden staircase – that has placed the *livraria* firmly on the list of the world's most beautiful bookshops.

The shop is basically an influencer's dream and no matter when you go, you'll struggle to get a shot without other people in it. Still, try to enjoy what makes this bookshop unique: the bulging bookshelves, the Art Nouveau struts and the busts of

SIGHTSEEING

INSIDER TIP
Offset your online ticket against a book

Portuguese writers. Just so you know, you can redeem the entrance fee (make sure you buy a ticket online in advance) against any books you buy. *Daily 9.30am–7pm | 8 euros | Rua das Carmelitas 144 | livrarialello.pt | buses and trams Carmo |* 📖 *h6*

9 UNIVERSIDADE DO PORTO

Porto's university was only founded in 1911 but, despite its relative youth, it is the country's second largest university, with a good 31,000 students enrolled here across 14 faculties. The 19th-century, Neoclassical, granite building previously housed the Academia Politécnica, which, like the medical school, was integrated into the newly founded Universidade do Porto.

If you want to take a look behind those imperviously thick walls, pay a visit to the university's *Museu de História Natural e da Ciência (entry from Jardim da Cordoaria | Tue–Sun 10am–1pm and 2–6pm | free admission at the time of going to press due to renovation work | mhnc.up.pt | ⏱ 45 mins)*. The collection includes pieces from the early days of teaching here, which began with a nautical school in 1762. *Campo dos Mártires da Pátria 81 | buses and trams Carmo |* 📖 *h6*

10 IGREJA DO CARMO & IGREJA DAS CARMELITAS

Porto is blessed with three attractions (and one major curiosity) linked to the Ordem do Carmo (Order of the Carmelites). The elaborate façades, and especially the side wall of the Igreja do Carmo, are adorned with *azulejos* that depict the founding history of the order on Mount Carmel. Now look closer: between the two churches is the narrowest building in

The slimline Torre dos Clérigos is visible from almost everywhere in Baixa

BAIXA

the city, the 1m-wide *Casa Escondida*! The Renaissance-style *Igreja dos Carmelitas* (left) was the first to exist, with building work commencing in 1620. Over time, its interior has been so lavishly adorned with Baroque and Rococo ornaments that it is hard to imagine the humble and unassuming monks who once prayed here. But by the 18th century, modesty was firmly out and the Carmelites set out to display their wealth and power on another level, meaning they needed a new, more representative church. The *Igreja do Carmo* (right) boasts a lavish Baroque façade with the four evangelists on the gable. To get into the Igreja do Carmo with its chambers and catacombs, you have to enter through the Casa Escondida. The house was actually built as a legal get-around. At the time, two churches were not allowed to stand directly next to one another. *Daily 9.30am–5pm, in summer until 6pm, closed for services | 5 euros | Rua do Carmo | FB: Turismo Ordem do Carmo Porto | buses and trams Carmo | ⏱ 20 mins | 📖 h6*

Below the cathedral is the once-neglected but now sought-after Bairro da Sé

11 BANCO DE MATERIAIS

Porto's "materials bank" is a kind of municipal archive where the city stores particularly decorative features from dilapidated buildings or buildings under renovation. Whether it's artistic tiles or stucco, wood and iron accessories or guttering, the aim is to preserve all this decorative architectural art. *Tue–Sun 10am–5.30pm | free admission | Praça de Carlos Alberto 71 | museudoporto.pt | buses and trams Carmo | ⏱ 20 mins | 📖 h6*

SIGHTSEEING

12 MUSEU NACIONAL DE SOARES DOS REIS 🌂

A very special art museum! The late 18th-century Palácio dos Carrancas today hides a pretty camellia garden tucked away at the back of the building. At one time it was home to the Mendes de Morais e Castro brothers, who ran a gold and silver braid factory on the premises. But in 1862, the royal family bought the property and since 1937 the palace has been a national museum, housing not only valuable furniture, musical instruments, jewellery and porcelain, but above all the works of the sculptor António Soares dos Reis. who was born near Porto in 1847. Tragically, the artist died from suicide in 1889 and it was only after his death that his talent began to be appreciated. Today he is recognised as one of the central figures of Portuguese realism. *Tue–Sun 10am–6pm | 5 euros | Rua Dom Manuel II 44 | museusoaresdosreis. gov.pt | buses Hospital Santo António | ⏱ 1 hr | 🗺 g6*

OLD TOWN

Porto's history began high above the river on the almost 80m-high granite hill of Pena Ventosa (meaning "windy rock") and on grey days the city can live up to its blustery reputation.

Where once the Celts had settled, the Romans followed. They arrived in the first century BCE, followed by Germanic peoples. After the Moorish period, the city became Catholic and, until the early 15th century, Porto was ruled by the bishops, who resided up here with the best views. In the 21st century, you can enjoy the area around the cathedral before heading into the *Bairro da Sé* district, just a stone's throw away. What was until recently a notorious no-go zone has now been successfully redeveloped. Alternatively, you can head down towards the river via Rua de Dom Hugo and the steep Escadas das Verdades; this will take you through the *Bairro do Barredo* down to the Ribeira riverside district with its narrow, colourful houses.

13 IGREJA DE SANTA CLARA

For years and years, this beautiful but little-known convent church was under renovation. Around 2.5 million euros and a whole decade later, the Igreja de Santa Clara has been given a new lease of life. Enter the courtyard of the former convent and everything looks deceptively simple: from the outside, this Gothic church gives no indication of the splendour that awaits inside. Once inside, the intricate *talha dourada* woodcarvings covered in fine gold leaf make it truly spectacular – a golden dream of angels, garlands, sculptures, columns, shells and swirls. The church is a testament to the reign of King João V in the 18th century, when so much of Porto's Baroque architecture came into being, and also to the country's colonial links with Brazil – after all, what would this church be without its precious Brazilian wood and gold? *Daily 9am–1pm, 2–6pm (except during*

OLD TOWN

services) | 3 euros | Largo 1° de Dezembro | metro São Bento | ⏱ 20 mins | ⏏ j7

🟥 TERREIRO DA SÉ

Today, the complex that consists of the cathedral, the bishop's palace, the pillory and the surrounding buildings is one harmonious historical ensemble. But the complex is actually a mishmash of many different eras. The oldest building is the ⭐ *Sé do Porto (daily 9am-5.30pm, April-Oct 9am-6.30pm | 3 euros, combi ticket with the Episcopal Palace 6 euros | ⏱ 30 mins)*, the cathedral itself, or more accurately its foundation walls, which date back to the 12th century. The rose window above the main entrance is all that remains of the original Roman Sé (the Portuguese word comes from the Latin *sede*, bishop's see). In the 18th century, the medieval fortified church was given a thoroughly Baroque makeover: Nicolau Nasoni added round domes to the mighty towers and relaxed the north façade with a pretty loggia.

Apart from the rose window, the interior is windowless, with highlights including the gilded main altar with its triumphal arch resting on spiral Solomonic columns and, in the left transept, the silver altar made from a whopping 700kg of silver! The 14th-century Gothic cloister was adorned with elaborate *azulejos* in the 18th century and leads the way to the cathedral, the treasury, the tower and the chapter house.

Right next door, the vast *Paço Episcopal (Mon-Sat 9am-1pm and 2-6pm | 4 euros, combi ticket with the Sé 6 euros | ⏱ 30 mins)* stands on the south side of the complex and houses the diocesan administration. The spacious square is dominated by the *Pelourinho*, an elaborately decorated pillory erected by the dictator Salazar in 1945, after he declared the square looked too empty following the demolition of other buildings. The *equestrian statue* of the knight Vímara Peres on the northern side of the Sé also dates back to the dictatorship and commemorates a hero of the ninth-century Reconquista.

The two stone cubes on the north side of the square might look old, but in fact they have been painted that way and are really the newest buildings on the square (although they do stand on medieval ruins). The lower tower, with the pseudo-historic battlements, houses a branch of the tourist information office. Behind the Sé, the recently opened stained-glass museum *Museu do Vitral (daily 10am-7pm | 8 euros incl. a glass of port | Rua de Dom Hugo 2-6 | museu dovitral.pt) is well worth visiting.*

Just a stone's throw away is a totally different world: at the foot of Terreiro da Sé lies the Old Town quarter of *Bairro da Sé*. Why not enjoy a leisurely stroll to explore? The tucked-away square of *Largo da Pena Ventosa* is especially idyllic. *Metro São Bento | ⏏ j7*

INSIDER TIP: From shabby to chic

🟥 FUNICULAR DOS GUINDAIS

So, you've seen the lower deck of the Ponte Dom Luís I up close but now

SIGHTSEEING

want to explore the top? We won't tell you how many steps that entails (up the Escadas do Codeçal, for example). Instead, save yourself the sweat and take the funicular up to Batalha Square. From the funicular you can also get a good look at the old city wall, the *Muralha Fernandina*, which protected the people of Porto and their cathedral in the 14th and 15th centuries.

INSIDER TIP: I spy the city wall

The last 90m of the 281m ascent take you through a tunnel. In the early 2000s, the decision was made to revive the route, which was more than 100 years old, with a modern funicular railway. The old railway had closed in 1893 following a serious accident just two years after its maiden voyage. Porto's current residents are thrilled with this new convenient way of overcoming the 60m climb. *April–Oct daily 8am–10pm, Fri/Sat 8am–midnight, Nov–March daily 8am–8pm, Fri/Sat 8am–10pm | 4 euros | buses Elevador Guindais | j7*

16 PONTE DOM LUÍS I ★

Without the world's largest wrought-iron arch in view, photos of the Ribeira, the river and the port cellars of Vila Nova de Gaia wouldn't be half as beautiful. This masterpiece is the work of Belgian Theóphile Seyrig, a student of Gustave Eiffel. Commissioned by King Luís I, the bridge was inaugurated In 1886, after five years of planning and construction. This was because Seyrig had to find a solution for the significant difference in height:

OLD TOWN

the Douro had cut deep into the rock. The distance between the lower and upper decks is 45m and the views from the top are just phenomenal. In total, the architect needed 3,000 tonnes of iron. The top deck is reserved for pedestrians and the metro, while cars can drive on the lower deck. The lower deck is also a favourite spot for fearless bridge-jumping kids, who plunge into the Douro near the south bank from a height of over 10m!

Despite its fame, the Ponte Dom Luís I was not the first bridge at this point: before its inauguration, the *Ponte Pênsil* suspension bridge was used to cross the river; two pillars on the Porto side stand testament to this history. Another bridge, the *Ponte das Barcas*, a bridge of wooden boats, collapsed under the weight of stampeding locals who were fleeing the Napoleonic invaders. A small wayside shrine near the first bars on the Ribeira commemorates this tragedy from 29 March 1809 and the 4,000 or so who died, known as the *alminhas da ponte*, or the "little souls of the bridge". *Buses Elevador Guindais | j7*

17 RIBEIRA ★

Day in, day out, countless photos are snapped of the colourful houses in Porto's traditional riverside district. There is a reason why these houses are so narrow. The trees for the crossbeams that supported the floors grew no taller than 6m or 7m – so the

Enjoy a view of the river from the Ribeira promenade – a perfect way to spend your holiday

SIGHTSEEING

houses went upwards but not outwards. Looking today at this spruced-up waterfront, it's hard to believe that not so very long ago, the Ribeira was a run-down dockland district that faced repeated flooding until a dam was built across the Douro. These days, you can enjoy your port cocktail in stylish terrace bars with a view of the river – dreamy! For cheaper eateries, head back up the hill away from the first row of restaurants.

What are presumed to be the city's oldest residential buildings, dating back to the 13th/14th century, can be found at 5 Rua de Baixo and 59 Rua da Reboleira. Another medieval building is the *Casa do Infante (Tue–Sun 10am–5.30pm | 4 euros,* 🐖 *combi ticket with other parts of the Museu do Porto 8 euros | museudoporto.pt |* ⏱ *1 hr),* which you can find at 10 Rua da Alfândega. In the 14th century, this building housed the customs office, a function which came with a great deal of prestige, as underpinned by the fact it not only served as a royal guesthouse and warehouse but also as the place where Philippa of Lancaster gave birth to her son Henry on 4 March 1394. Henry would go down in history as Prince Henry the Navigator and one of the primary figures in Portugal's Golden Age of Discovery. The interactive museum also covers the history and development of Porto more generally, with Roman floor mosaics and a scale model of the medieval city on display.

From here, walk to the water's edge and you will reach Cais da Estiva. To the west, the narrow wall path is called *Muro dos Bacalhoeiros* and is where the cod traders once unloaded their fishy cargo. From here, head to the lower entrance of the 🏴 *Museu do Vinho do Porto (Tue-Sun 10am–5.30pm | 4 euros,* 🐖 *combi ticket with other parts of the Museu do Porto 8 euros | museudoporto.pt |* ⏱ *45 mins).* Enjoy a port tasting at the bar before discovering the four narrow floors and the stories they tell of the city and its role in the port wine trade.

Goods used to be hauled off ships and loaded onto ox-drawn carts on the medieval *Praça da Ribeira*; today water cascades from the "floating" bronze cube that is the *Fonte do Cubo* fountain. In the year 2000, the sometimes-misunderstood sculptor João Cutileiro immortalised Porto's patron saint John the Baptist here in marble as a benign shepherd – all that's missing are the glasses to complete the bearded hipster vibes.

> **INSIDER TIP**
> **The coolest of saints**

Turn the corner and the winding alleys lead to *Bairro do Barredo*. If you can't face the steps, take the free glass lift 🐖 *Ascensor da Ribeira (daily 8am–8pm, open later in summer and at the weekend),* also called *Elevador da Lada*: The lift was opened in 1994 to link Largo dos Arcos da Ribeira to a scenic connecting bridge some 30m higher. Head through the stairwell of the building to reach the Escadas do Barredo which then lead breezily downhill or further up towards the cathedral. *Buses Ribeira | 📖 h–j7*

> **INSIDER TIP**
> **A shortcut of glass**

41

OLD TOWN

🔸 IGREJA DE SÃO FRANCISCO

Originally built between the 13th and 15th centuries as a simple Gothic church for the modest Franciscan friars, the Igreja de São Franciso was given a truly blingy makeover in the rather more opulent 18th-century style. Take a deep breath and prepare to be blown away by at least 300kg of gold leaf. Back in the 18th century, the wealthy families of Porto hoped to buy their salvation with generous donations to finance this Baroque bling. Their reward? To be buried in the adjoining catacombs after their death. Today their bones lie in the *ossário*, the ossuary, interspersed with the remains of the (one would hope!) pious monks. *Daily 9am–7pm, April–Sept 9am–8pm | 9 euros | Rua da Bolsa 80 | ordemsaofrancisco.pt | tram 1 Infante | ⏱ 30 mins | 📖 h7*

🔸 PALÁCIO DA BOLSA ⭐

This building means business, literally. In Porto, it was the bourgeois merchants, not the monarchs, who called the shots. The Stock Exchange Palace was and is the most magnificent building in the city. While the spectacular trading floor is no longer trodden by pacing brokers (they decamped to Lisbon) but instead by awestruck visitors, the building still houses the Porto Chamber of Commerce. In fact, it was the Chamber's members who financed the stunning Neoclassical building, the construction of which took over 70 years and was only completed in 1909. The wonderfully opulent marble and granite staircase alone took 40 years to complete! The sheer extravagance of the building is incredible: some of the chandeliers weigh an entire tonne and the Arabian Room is designed to make traders feel as if they have been transported to the Andalusian Alhambra. If you happen to be there around lunchtime, try out the adjoining restaurant *O Comercial (closed Mon lunchtime and Sun | tel. 9 18 83 86 49 | ocomercial.com | €€)* for upmarket food with a view.

INSIDER TIP: Lunch with bankers and traders

During the week, the lunch menu is a reasonable 23 euros. *Guided tours only (including in English) daily 9am–6.30pm | 12 euros | Rua de Ferreira Borges | palaciodabolsa.com | tram 1 Infante | ⏱ 45 mins | 📖 h7*

🔸 MUSEU DAS MARIONETAS

This small museum brings the world of puppet theatre to life with everything from creative hand puppets and props for a Punch and Judy show to elaborate, almost life-sized marionettes. Visitors are invited to touch some of the figures made of wood, papier-mâché and other materials and discover how they are made. The museum works closely with the puppet theatre next door and many of the puppets crop up in their shows, as you will see in the videos showing the rehearsals and puppet shows! *Wed–Sun 2–6pm, Sat/Sun also 11am–1pm | 3.50 euros, children 2.50 euros | Rua de Belomonte 61 | marionetasdoporto.pt | tram 1, buses 403, 500, 910 Infante | ⏱ 30 mins | 📖 h7*

SIGHTSEEING

Porto's Stock Exchange, the Palácio da Bolsa, is the most magnificent building in the city

21 ALFÂNDEGA NOVA

With the inauguration of the New Customs House in 1869, the medieval fishing district of Miragaia ("view of Gaia") lost not only its view of Gaia but also its beach, which had become a harbour. But the economic boom didn't last: the construction of the port in Leixões saw the hulking customs building on the banks of the Douro sink into insignificance. Luckily, Porto's star architect Eduardo Souto de Moura breathed new life into the building in the 1990s. Since then, it has housed an events and conference centre alongside the *Museu dos Transportes e Comunicações (Tue–Fri 10am–1pm and 2–6pm, Sat/Sun 3–7pm | 3 euros | amtc.pt)*. The museum, which is well worth a visit, offers permanent and temporary exhibitions telling the story of transport and communications, including a collection of carriages and state coaches used by Portugal's presidents. You can also visit the free, permanent exhibition on remodelling the customs building. *Rua Nova da Alfândega | Buses and trams Alfândega | 1 hr | g7*

22 WORLD OF DISCOVERIES

Whether the World of Discoveries is a romanticised glorification of the "golden age" of Portuguese voyages or just another interactive history museum is open to debate. Still, one thing is for sure: kids will love the boat trip that traces the voyages of the

43

PORTO WEST

PORTO WEST

Much of the sprawling west side of Porto has long since been gentrified: with magnificent views around most corners and romantic estates and parks, the area might come as a surprise.

Thanks to the Atlantic, you can usually feel a fresh breeze here, at least fresher than in the working and industrial districts to east of the city. Of course, it made sense for Porto's elite to build their homes here. That said, in the late 18th century, foundries, ceramics manufacturers, furniture factories and others were established here, down by the river, in what used to be the rural fishing suburb of Massarelos.

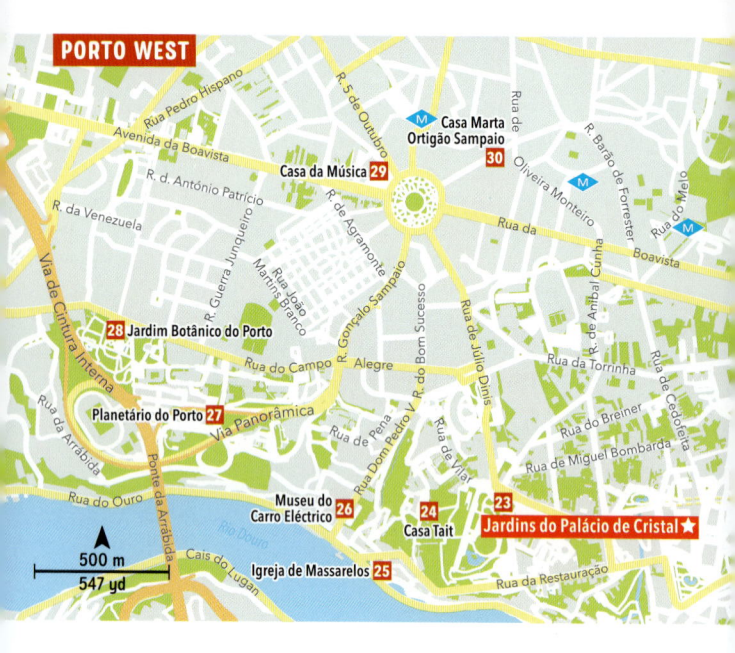

great Portuguese navigators and explorers. It certainly is a fun way to explore the globe: the family sets off in a small boat to sail around the African continent to India and Brazil, learning all about the legendary seafarers of the 15th and 16th centuries along the way. Parents, for their part, might want to take the opportunity to draw their children's attention to the less-than-pleasant aspects of these voyages and their impact on indigenous peoples in an age-appropriate way – something the museum conveniently glazes over. *Tue–Fri 10am–6pm, Sat/Sun 10am–7pm | 16 euros, children (aged 4–12) 10 euros | Rua de Miragaia 106 | worldofdiscoveries.com | tram and buses Alfândega |* ⏱ *1½ hrs|* 📖 *g7*

SIGHTSEEING

In fact, you can still see traces of these industries today. As a result, the wealthy *portuenses* moved higher and further west. Boavista is another of the city's more refined western neighbourhoods: towards the end of the 19th century, what had once been rural settlements quickly became trendy residential hotspots. The result? Wide avenues and spacious squares with modern office and hotel buildings dotted in between. Arrábida, for its part, offers magnificent parks, while the students of the more modern faculties located here keep the cafés busy.

23 JARDINS DO PALÁCIO DE CRISTAL ★

If you were asked to name Porto's most beautiful gardens, you'd struggle to top the "crystal palace gardens". This large park really does have it all: from linden-lined avenues to meadows, ponds and truly spectacular views, where winding paths lead to the precipice high above the banks of the Douro and small turrets serve as romantic *miradouros*. The gardens were designed by German landscape architect Émile David who created many a romantic garden in Porto in the 19th century.

The park owes its name to the crystal palace built here for the first industrial exhibition in 1865. The original was replaced by a round sports palace in 1951, and in 1991 the multi-purpose venue was renamed *Pavilhão Rosa Mota* in honour of Porto's beloved long-distance runner and Olympic champion. Today, it is a modern concert venue. For a spot of Romance, head to the *Museu Romântico (Tue–Sun 10am–5.30pm | 4 euros, combi ticket with other branches of the Museu do Porto 8 euros | Rua de Entre Quintas 220 | museudoporto.pt | 1 hr)* in the former Quinta da Macierinha. Over two floors, the museum's many rooms tell the story of Romanticism in Porto and reveal how an aristocratic family would have lived in the 19th century, complete with Empire-style decorations, playful furniture and elegant tableware. *Daily 8am–7pm, summer 8am–9pm | free entry | Rua Dom Manuel II | buses Palácio | 1 hr | F–G6*

24 CASA TAIT

Follow the cobblestone lane Rua de Entre Quintas and at the top you'll find the former estate of the port merchant William Tait. Skip to the present day, and the rooms of the mansion now house the offices of the Museu do Porto, with a beautiful view of the magnificent garden. And you don't have to work there to visit the garden for free and enjoy the stunning views towards the river and the seemingly endless greenery (including the ivy-clad villa itself). Don't miss the more than 250-year-old tulip tree – a spectacular natural monument. Visit in winter (January/February) to see the camellia trees in full bloom. *Mon–Fri 7.30am–7.30pm | free entry | Rua de Entre Quintas 219 | museudoporto.pt | buses Palácio | 20 mins | F6*

PORTO WEST

25 IGREJA DE MASSARELOS

Nestled in the old streets of Massarelos, the Igreja do Corpo Santo de Massarelos is so much more than a simple parish chapel; it is the headquarters of the oldest brotherhood in Porto. It was founded in 1394 by rescued seafarers. Later, in the 15th century, Henry the Navigator was a member of the brotherhood; check out the deep blue *azulejo* panel on the side facing the river to see him alongside St Erasmus (São Telmo), the protector of seafarers. The saint is also depicted as a wooden figure in the niche above the entrance portal of the now-renovated church. Today, the brotherhood numbers some 80 members whose current mission is less about protecting seafarers and more about taking care of the museum, where the most valuable piece is a cloak embroidered with gold and silver thread that Queen Maria I presented to the *confraria* in 1790. *April–Sept Mon–Sat 10am–noon, 2–6pm, Oct–March Mon–Sat 2–6pm | museum 2 euros, church free | Largo do Adro | confraria corposantomassarelos.pt | tram 1 Cais das Pedras | ⓧ 20 mins | ⎕ F6*

26 MUSEU DO CARRO ELÉCTRICO 🎭

The old steam power station in Massarelos boasts an excellently preserved machine room and is well worth a visit in its own right. From 1915, the plant was responsible for generating the power for Porto's electric trams. These days, it houses retired tram carriages, the oldest of which date back to 1872 and would have been horse-drawn. Porto's first electric tram arrived in the city in 1905. As an added bonus, visitors can climb aboard some of the carriages. Just one word of warning! Your little one may well leave the museum with a new ambition in life: tram driver! *Tue–Sun 10am–6pm | 8 euros, children and young people (aged 6–25) 4 euros | Alameda Basílio Teles 51 | museudocarroelectrico.pt | trams and buses Museu Carro Eléctrico | ⓧ 50 mins | ⎕ E–F6*

27 PLANETÁRIO DO PORTO 🎭

The best spot in Porto for stargazing. This university-run astrophysics centre houses a state-of-the-art digital projection system that reveals the solar system to visitors. You can marvel at thousands of stars and lose yourself in distant galaxies. Themed sessions cover different aspects of astronomy (see website), so you can choose your time slot. *Daily 2–5pm | 5 euros, children 3.50 euros | Rua das Estrelas | planetario.up.pt | buses Faculdade Arquitetura | ⓧ 1 hr | ⎕ E5*

28 JARDIM BOTÂNICO DO PORTO 🐾🎭

Porto's botanical garden comes as something of a surprise. Apart from the odd student, few people venture into these magnificent grounds, repurposed by the university as a botanical garden in 1951. And that is despite the fact it costs absolutely nothing to get in! Wonderful old trees and a number of themed gardens complement beautifully restored greenhouses from the 1960s and an impressive collection of cacti.

SIGHTSEEING

The one drawback is the garden's proximity to the motorway – the traffic noise can put a bit of a dampener on the mood in the lower part of the gardens at certain times of day. Still, the Brazilian – the Quinta do Campo worlds, even for kids. *Daily 9am–6pm, in summer until 7pm | free entry | Rua do Campo Alegre 1191 | jardim botanico.up.pt | buses Jardim Botânico | ⏱ 1 hr | ▥ D5*

Public transport through the ages: Museu do Carro Eléctrico

Alegre – who built his palace here in 1875 could hardly have foreseen that! In the late 19th century, the wealthy Danish-Portuguese Andresen family acquired the property, renovated the *quinta* and "romanticised" the park.

Today, the stately Casa Andresen houses the 🔭 *Galeria da Biodiversidade (Tue–Sun 10am–1pm and 2–6pm | 5 euros, children aged 5–17 2.50 euros | mhnc.up.pt | ⏱ 1 hr)*, a science museum with interactive exhibits on the topic of biodiversity. Plus, there are always exciting temporary exhibitions that open the door to fascinating new

🎵 CASA DA MÚSICA 🎭 ⭐

The people of Porto are proud of their postmodern "house of music" – and rightly so! Widely regarded as Portugal's top concert venue, the space boasts an impressive cultural programme. It's just what you'd expect from a venue that is home to three in-house ensembles and a choir as well as hosting plenty of guest musicians. And did we mention that the acoustics were outstanding? The venue is testament to the work of the team of architects led by Rem Koolhaas from Rotterdam. Tours of the building explain why certain colours

FOZ DO DOURO

and materials were chosen, why the main hall features a glass wall facing the city, and how it was possible to achieve the same acoustic experience from every seat in the hall named after Porto-born cellist Guilhermina Suggia (1885–1950).

Concerts in the rectangular hall are relatively affordable as the acoustics are just as good no matter where you sit, and so every ticket costs the same. It's also worth keeping an eye out for concerts or events in Sala 2, Cibermúsica, or in fact any other corner of the labyrinthine building, as you might just stumble across a mind-blowing experimental gig. Be sure to visit the shop while you're here as they sell beautiful and unusual music-themed souvenirs! *Guided tours (in English) Wed and Fri-Mon 11am and daily at 4pm | 12 euros (option to deduct from the cost of a concert ticket) | Avenida da Boavista 604 | casadamusica.com | metro Casa da Música | ⓘ 1 hr | ⌘ F4*

> **INSIDER TIP**
> **Souvenirs with a musical twist**

🎟 CASA MARTA ORTIGÃO SAMPAIO ☂

This late 1950s modernist house doesn't look like a museum. And if it weren't for the sign at the entrance, you probably would walk straight on by. Home to the collection of painter and art patron Marta Ortigão Sampaio (1891–1978), this museum is still a real insider tip as hardly anyone visits. And yet there are all kinds of valuable paintings, jewellery and furniture inside the museum, which spans a whopping six floors. It's the perfect place to while away an hour or so on a rainy afternoon. And if the sun appears, you'll find the loveliest green garden outside. *Tue–Sun 10am–5.30pm | 4 euros, 🐷 combi ticket with other branches of the Museu do Porto 8 euros | Rua de Nossa Senhora de Fátima 291–299 | museudoporto.pt | metro Carolina Michaëlis | ⓘ 1 hr | ⌘ G4*

FOZ DO DOURO

A crisp Atlantic breeze ensures good air quality in the so-called "mouth of the Douro", Porto's westernmost district.

When the age of industrialisation, and with it stinking great factories, arrived in the east of the city, wealthy *portuenses* moved further and further west. As well as the fresh air here, there was plenty of space to build lavish villas and ample opportunity to stroll along the green banks of the river or the wide Atlantic promenade.

And so, in the 19th century, this former fishing district was transformed into the city's most elegant quarter, enjoying a reputation as a fashionable seaside resort. Even today, plenty of holidaymakers are happy to stay here near the Atlantic. After all, the historic E1 tram or the city buses will quickly whisk you to the area around the early 18th-century Baroque parish church of São João da Foz do Douro and, for

SIGHTSEEING

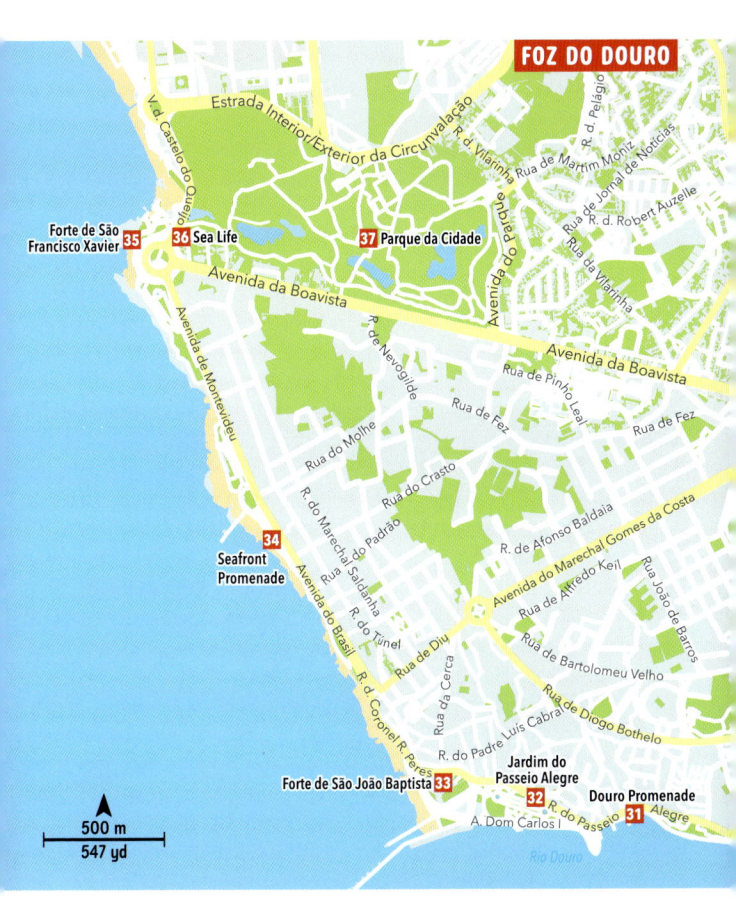

those hoping for some old-town flair, to the picturesque cobblestone alleys in *Foz Velha*, the old Foz.

31 DOURO PROMENADE

The promenade of Foz do Douro begins, at the very latest, at the point where the Ribeira da Granja stream flows into the Douro. We recommend you head for the small riverside park of *Jardim do Calém*, where an attractive iron bench is almost begging you to sit and watch the birds. Just next door is the *Jardim das Sobreiras*. Pause to sip a *galão* in one of the two cafés with a view while you let your children loose on the snaking paths of the park. From here you can already see the small headland that stretches a few metres further into the estuary of the Douro. This is the site of the *Farol de São Miguel-o-Anjo*, a square lighthouse-cum-chapel and Portugal's first Renaissance building. It is, in fact,

FOZ DO DOURO

the oldest lighthouse in the country and has been guiding boats for almost 500 years! Meanwhile, the *Marégrafo*, right at the tip of the headland, has been measuring the tides and water levels since the late 19th century. *Tram 1 Fluvial oder Passeio Alegre | d5*

32 JARDIM DO PASSEIO ALEGRE

In Porto, if you come across an exquisite, late 19th-century park, the chances are it will have been designed by Émile David. Indeed, the German landscape architect was also responsible for this most beautiful of gardens in Foz do Douro. The romantic *Chalé Suiço*, the "Swiss Chalet", was built in 1874 and makes for a dreamy pitstop with plenty of snacks, coffee and drinks available. You can get your strength up here before taking to the course just around the corner at the *Clube de Minigolfe do Porto (summer Mon–Fri 10am–8pm, Sat/Sun 9am–8pm, winter Tue–Fri 10am–6pm, Sat/Sun 10am–7pm | 3 euros, children 1.50 euros)*.

> **INSIDER TIP**
> **Tee off in a romantic park**

The course is shady and well kept, not to mention very competitively priced! *Tram 1 Passeio Alegre | c5*

33 FORTE DE SÃO JOÃO BAPTISTA

This powerful and somewhat intimidating fortress towers between estuary and the Atlantic. Construction started in the 16th century to ward off pirates, and to this day a regional military unit is stationed within the thick walls … right next to the tennis club. Despite this, the grounds are at times open to the public *(usually Mon–Fri 9am–5pm)*. From the fortress, it's just a few steps to the two breakwater moles on the northern bank of the Douro estuary.

> **INSIDER TIP**
> **Stroll out to sea**

Waves and wind permitting, you can wander along them for a wonderful view. In 1886, the outermost point of the older, shorter mole was topped with a hexagonal, 10m-high lighthouse, the *Farolim de Felgueiras*. Today, it is no longer in use, having been replaced by an adjoining more modern, 500m-long mole and the Leça da Palmeira lighthouse. *Esplanada do Castelo | bus 500 Praia do Ourigo | c5*

34 SEAFRONT PROMENADE

Porto's seafront promenade starts at the estuary breakwaters and offers every opportunity for the perfect walk (or even swim, in summer): it is varyingly a footpath and cyclepath, a wooden walkway through sandy coves, a stretch shaded by trees and a route past beachside cafés. The delicately yellow-washed, semicircular *Pérgola da Foz* certainly wins the prize for "most romantic spot"; who knows how many of Porto's citizens have proposed here! Wander a little further along the beach to the sandy area and the *homem do leme*, the "man at the helm". A bronze monument has adorned the park behind the beach in honour of the nation's helmsmen since 1934 – a nod to Portugal's long history as a land of explorers and seafarers. It was even the theme of a hit song by rock band Xutos & Pontapés. *Bus 500 several stops | b–c 3–5*

50

SIGHTSEEING

Visit the Forte São Francisco Xavier I for the wonderful views from the terrace

35 FORTE DE SÃO FRANCISCO XAVIER

Forte de São Francisco Xavier is known locally as "cheese castle", or *Castelo do Queijo*, thanks to the granite rocks, pitted by eons of erosion, on which it has stood since the mid-17th century. An older defensive structure predated the current fort and, if you are interested in its history, you can visit the small museum, with exhibitions on the Napoleonic and Miguelist Wars of the 19th century. Also inside is a viewing terrace, where you can drink in the magnificent view of the old cannons and along the coast as far as the modern cruise terminal of Matosinhos. *Tue-Sun 9am-6pm | 0.50 euros | Praça de Gonçalves Zarco | buses 500, 502 Castelo do Queijo | b3*

36 SEA LIFE

If the heavens open, families can always rely on a trip to the aquarium, and this one certainly boasts a vast underwater world, with 31 tanks and some 3,000 creatures. The sharks, rays and penguins are all surefire hits.

INSIDER TIP: Fish food — Try to catch feeding time for extra action! *Core hours daily 10am-6pm | 16.50 euros, children (aged 3-12) 11.50 euros | Praça de Gonçalves Zarco | visitsealife.com | buses 500, 502 Castelo do Queijo | 2-3 hrs | b3*

37 PARQUE DA CIDADE

Completed only in 2002, this urban park is the country's largest – and is a veritable paradise for joggers, cyclists, footballers or just anyone out for a walk. Winding paths lead through the gently undulating forest and parkland past lakes, sports fields and small *miradouros*. If the sun is shining, you can reckon on finding a crowd, especially on a Sunday afternoon, when

VILA NOVA DE GAIA

the people of Porto flock to their park for family picnics or children's birthdays. In early June, a section of the park is taken over for the alternative music festival *NOS Primavera Sound*. Worth visiting in the northern end of the park is the interactive science museum 🐒 *Pavilhão da Água (April–Oct Tue–Sun, Nov–March Mon–Sat 9.30am–12.30pm and 1.30–5.30pm | 8 euros, children (aged 4–12) 5 euros | Estrada da Circunvalação 15443 | pavilhaodaagua.pt | bus 205 Parque da Cidade | ⏱ 1 hr)*. The museum covers everything you need to know about water and the environment, including hydropower. 📖 *b–c 2–3*

VILA NOVA DE GAIA

If you cross the iron Ponte Dom Luís I, you'll find yourself in neighbouring Vila Nova de Gaia, which, with a population of 300,000, is actually bigger than Porto itself.

In the historic "Old Gaia", at the foot of the rocky Serra do Pilar, you won't notice any modern city buzz. Here, everything revolves around port, which is stored in the shady Douro slopes in *caves* (wine cellars) where it slowly matures. Most of the port caves offer tours and tastings.

If you want to discover the residential areas of Gaia, take the A1 or A20 motorway south. The closer you get to the beaches of the Atlantic, the higher the density of villas; a cyclepath runs parallel to the fine beaches of Gaia and past the wealthy seaside suburbs.

38 MOSTEIRO DA SERRA DO PILAR

If you've been wondering where you can snap the best photos of Porto and the Ponte Dom Luís I, here's your answer! Construction started on the former Augustinian monastery in 1537 and lasted more than 70 years. The monastery is located on the hill of Serra do Pilar, the prime location for views over the Douro. Take the route along the upper part of the bridge and you'll reach the monastery forecourt from the cathedral hill in just a few minutes. Sadly, the monastery itself is not currently open to visitors. *Largo do Avis | metro Jardim do Morro | 📖 j8*

39 JARDIM DO MORRO

Both locals and tourists have delighted in the crescent-shaped hill park right next to the Mosteiro da Serra do Pilar since 1927. While some come to picnic by the romantic lake, for an after-work beer in the terrace café or to play cards, others sit on the panoramic benches and snap away for their Instagram stories – in their defence, this is where you'll find some of the most breathtaking views of Porto, especially of the picturesque Ribeira district. The cable car, however, is strictly for tourists; the locals save themselves the money and prefer to walk quickly through the labyrinthine alleys down to the city centre. The *Teleférico de Gaia (every day 10am–6pm, summer until 7 or 8pm | 7 euros, 10 euros for a return ticket |*

SIGHTSEEING

gaiacablecar.com) takes five minutes to glide over the roofs of the port cellars to the riverbank 60m below. *Metro Jardim do Morro* | j8

40 PORT CELLARS ★

Most of the port cellars here offer tours as well as the chance to sample their wares, meaning you can fully immerse yourself in the world of fortified wine! Just behind the Ponte Dom Luís I, *Burmester (daily 10am-1pm and 2-7pm | 15 euros incl. tasting | Largo Dom Luís I | tel. 9 13 28 89 94 | burmester.pt/caves)* is the first to offer an hour-long tour. Just above the riverbank, 300-year-old *Taylor's (daily 11am-6pm | 20 euros incl. tasting | Rua do Choupelo 250 | tel. 2 23 77 29 73 | taylor.pt)* offers a more extensive two-hour tour complete with audio guide and explanatory videos. Over at *Sandeman (daily 10am-12.30pm and 2-6pm | 19 euros incl. tasting | Largo Miguel Bombarda 47 | tel. 2 23 74 05 34 | sandeman.com)*, which was founded by a Scot in 1790, a virtual "Don", complete with the trademark black cloak, will guide you through the winery. If you're not too bothered about a tour but are just hankering after a delicious Cruz Pink Mojito with what might just be the best view of Porto, head for the rooftop bar *Terrace Lounge 360° (Tue-Sat 12.30pm-midnight, Sun 12.30-7pm | Largo Miguel Bombarda | espaco portocruz.pt)*, which belongs to *Espaço Porto Cruz*. h-j8

INSIDER TIP: A port cocktail and a view

53

VILA NOVA DE GAIA

Porto's elixir is stored in the cellars of Vila Nova de Gaia

41 CAIS DE GAIA

Some glide down in a cable car from Jardim do Morro, others arrive at Gaia's riverside promenade via the lower part of the Ponte Dom Luís I (pausing in summer to admire the fearless kids jumping off the bridge into the water below), while yet others disembark from a river cruise along the Douro. The fact is, no matter how you get there, there is always something going on along the riverbank of Gaia, with its countless cafés, port tastings and wine boutiques.

The old *barcos rabelos*, the attractive wooden boats once used to transport precious port barrels from the Douro Valley to the cellars of Gaia, have now become a perfect photo opportunity. Of course, these days the job falls to lorries, and the boats only really come into their own once a year during the city festival, when they become regatta boats. Head to the western end of the riverside promenade, past the restaurant zone, to see the small shipyard there; the last one where these boats are still built, repaired and of course readied for those tourist snaps. *Buses 901, 906 Largo de Aljubarrota* | h8

INSIDER TIP
Check out this tiny shipyard

42 CONVENTO DE CORPUS CHRISTI

Tucked away among all the port cellars, art lovers can seek out this former Dominican convent, now a municipal cultural centre with changing exhibitions. The octagonal convent church is richly decorated with *talha dourada*;

SIGHTSEEING

more spectacular still are the walnut carvings and colourful paintings that adorn the chancel.

The convent, which was founded in the 14th century, was originally located right by the river. Fortunately for the nuns, who regularly found they had wet feet and sodden belongings, a more flood-proof, Baroque building was built a little higher up in the 17th century. *Mon-Fri 9.30am-1pm and 2-5.30pm | free entry | Largo de Aljubarrota 13 | buses 901, 906 Largo de Aljubarrota | ⏱ 20 mins | 🚌 h8*

43 WORLD OF WINE
Opened in 2020 in renovated old port wine warehouses, World of Wine (WOW) houses a complex of seven museums, as well as restaurants, bars, shops and a wine school. Unsurprisingly, the focus falls on wine and port, but there is also plenty to discover about the history of Porto, Portuguese cork, chocolate and its 5,000-year history, historical drinking vessels, and fashion and design in the Porto region. *Daily 10am-7pm | 20-65 euros depending on the number of museums visited | Rua do Choupelo 39 | wow.pt | buses 901, 906 Choupelo | 🚌 H8*

44 LOOK AT PORTO 🎭
If you're only on a fleeting visit to Porto, this interactive 5D cinema could be a good option. The wind blows through your hair as you sit on a tram and whizz round the "city", including some unusual views. The shop sells some good souvenirs. *Daily 10am-8pm | 9 euros, children (aged 5-11) 6 euros | Largo Joaquim Magalhães 12 | lookatporto.pt | metro D Jardim do Morro | ⏱ 20 mins | 🚌 H8*

OTHER SIGHTS

45 CAPELA SANTA CATARINA
The view here really is an insider tip, especially at sunset! Admittedly, it's not easy to find this whitewashed chapel in the parish of Lordelo de Ouro, hidden away as it is among the houses on a hill. But once you've tackled the ascent, a magnificent view opens up towards the estuary and the Atlantic. King João I chose this hill, which was easily visible from the water at the time and well outside the city gates, as the site of a chapel for Porto's sailors in honour of their patron saint, Catherine. *Irregular opening hours | Largo de Santa Catarina 3 | bus 207 Santa Catarina | 🚌 C5*

46 PARQUE DE SERRALVES ⭐
If you love contemporary art and architecture and yet also seek a connection to nature, you absolutely must visit the grounds of the Serralves Foundation. Its *Museu de Arte Contemporânea*, built by Álvaro Siza Vieira and inaugurated in 1999, offers the most acclaimed international exhibitions in the country. The asymmetrical building alone is sensational, boasting cool and yet light-flooded corridors and 11 halls of

OTHER SIGHTS

different sizes – the green of the park never out of sight.

In the park, you'll find *Casa Serralves*, which offers yet more space for exhibitions. In 1925, francophile textile manufacturer Carlos Alberto Cabral commissioned this delicate pink Art Deco villa – and, of course, the phenomenal, stepped gardens at its feet. Today, most people consider the estate to be the finest example of Art Deco architecture in Portugal. Back in its day, all the most famous designers participated; for example, the skylight first-floor hall was created by the French jewellery and glass artist René Lalique. The renovation of the Casa Serralves was led by Álvaro Siza Vieira, who also converted the former garage into the *Casa do Cinema Manoel de Oliveira*. The latter is dedicated to the world of film, and in particular to the legendary director Manoel de Oliveira (1908–2015) who, you guessed it, came from Porto.

After all that indoor culture, make sure you take time to explore the vast park. The entire Serralves property spans a total of 18 hectares, with plenty of sculptures by renowned artists along the way. Some of the trees here date back to the 19th century; the 260m-long *Treetop Walkway* guides visitors through a part of the forest – in places at a height of 15m! Back on the ground, you can grab a quick bite at the wisteria-decked pergola of the cosy *Casa de Chá*. The park also hosts fabulous cultural events – *Jazz no Parque* and *Serralves em Festa* both come highly recommended. *April–Sept Mon–Fri 10am–7pm, Sat/Sun 10am–8pm, Oct–March Mon–Fri 10am–6pm, Sat/Sun 10am–7pm | park and all three museums 20 euros (park only/1 museum only 13 euros) | Rua Dom João de Castro 210 | serralves.pt | buses 203, 207 Serralves | ½ day | B3–4, d4*

INSIDER TIP
Treetop adventure

47 ESTÁDIO DO DRAGÃO

FC Porto is one of the three most important football clubs in the country, and the *dragões*, with their blue and white strip, regularly feature in European fixtures too. Football fans should be sure to visit the hallowed turf, the locker rooms and the club museum *Museu Futebol Clube do Porto (Mon 2.30–7pm, Tue–Sun 10am–7pm)* in the 2003 Dragon Stadium. Stadium tours are available with an

SIGHTSEEING

English-language audio guide (but not on home match days or the day before a UEFA game!) *Mon 3–5pm, Tue–Sun 11am–5pm on the hour | 15 euros | Via Futebol Clube do Porto | fcporto.pt | metro Estádio do Dragão |* ⏱ *1½ hrs|* 📖 *N3*

48 MUSEU NACIONAL DA IMPRENSA

Visitors with kids won't regret heading out to Ponte do Freixo to explore this museum of printing, where old printing techniques are brought back to life. *Closed until 2025 (provisionally) | N 108 206 (behind the Ponte do Freixo) | museudaimprensa.pt | buses 400, ZC Senhora da Hora |* 📖 *O7*

AROUND PORTO

49 SÃO PEDRO DA AFURADA

4km west of Vila Nova de Gaia / 20 mins by bike along the river

If you're on the hunt for the *real* Portugal, head to this community with a population of just 3,500 on the southern bank of the Douro. Here, life still largely revolves around fishing boats, fishing bars and fishing festivals. Many of the 19th-century houses feature walls decorated with tiles depicting boats or saints, which are said to protect the boats. Some housewives still tend to their washing by hand in the *lavadouro público*, or community washhouse, and enjoy a chat with their neighbours to boot. The

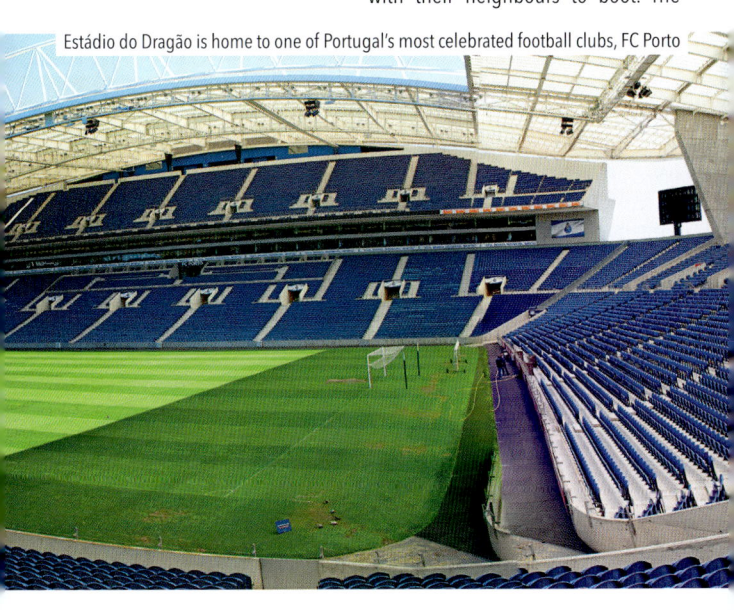

Estádio do Dragão is home to one of Portugal's most celebrated football clubs, FC Porto

57

AROUND PORTO

The aqueduct in Vila do Condo once had 99 arches, but only a few remain intact

laundry drying outside on quite precarious washing poles makes for some great arty photos.

If you're bristling at the use of the term "housewife", you can head for the 🐟 *Centro Interpretativo do Patriomónio da Afurada (daily 10am–12.30pm and 1.30–6pm | free entry | Rua António dos Santos 10 | parquebiologico.pt/cipa/o-centro-interpretativo | ⏱ 20 mins)* where the role of women in these fishing families is just one of the topics explored. Religion, tradition and fishing techniques all feature too. The yellow village bakery *Padaria 1° de Maio (Mon–Sat 7am–1pm and 3–8pm, Sun 7.30am–1pm | Rua Agostinho Albano 68)* of course features beautiful blue and white *azulejos* and is the perfect place to stop for a coffee; treat yourself to a mouthwatering pastry or snack too.

If you're ready for some sea views, the *Estuário do Douro*, a nature conservation zone, is just 2km away; it is a vast sand dune beach and bird sanctuary, ideal for birdwatching. And just on one side, there you have it: the Atlantic Ocean! Dive into the waves at Gaia's first beach, *Praia de Lavadores*. The beachside café *A Mar (open daily in summer 9am–9pm, winter Tue–Sun 9am–8pm | Avenida Beira Mar 896 | tel. 2 20 99 25 19 | FB: amarcafebar | €€)* is a space not just for taking in the sea air, but also for poetry and literature. Its small library offers plenty of reading material. A glass of cool white port and a crisp salad will round off the experience.

São Pedro da Afurada is well worth a quick look. You can check it out on a bike, or else bus 902 will take you close to the town and to Praia de Lavadores. 📖 *A–C 6–8*

58

SIGHTSEEING

50 PRAIA DO SENHOR DA PEDRA
14km south of Porto / 20 mins by local train from Campanhã to Miramar

INSIDER TIP — Cameras at the ready!

This hexagonal chapel that crowns a rock lapped by the sea at the heart of a bright sandy beach might just be *the* photo of your trip. The 18th-century chapel is a stunning choice for a day at the beach. Plus, you will be spoilt for choice with places to eat and drink right by the beach, including something for every budget. 📖 *I1*

51 VILA DO CONDE
27km northwest of Porto / 45 mins on the metro from Trindade to Vila do Conde (Santa Clara)

The imposing Santa Clara Monastery towers over the pretty Vila do Conde, between the Rio Ave and the Atlantic Ocean. Work started on the religious building in 1318, on the site of a Roman fort, and was later followed by the count's castle. Potential plans are underway to transform the now-empty monastery into a hotel. Until then, you can admire the remaining arches of what used to be a 7km-long aqueduct (originally with 999 arches), built in the 18th century to channel water from the mountains near Póvoa de Varzim, north of Porto, to the monastery well.

Wander along the banks of the Rio Ave and you will soon pass the *Alfândega Régia (Tue–Sun 10am–6pm | 2 euros | Largo da Alfândega),* the royal customs building dating from 1487. Today, it houses a maritime and shipbuilding museum. Your ticket also allows you to look around the *Nau Quinhentista,* a replica of a 16th-century sailing ship, opposite. Try to imagine what it was like for the Portuguese sailors discovering the world on a ship just like this one.

INSIDER TIP — Life on board, 16th-century style

Directly behind the museum is the *Capela do Socorro*; with its white domes and beautiful 18th-century *azulejos*. Further south, by the mouth of the estuary, is the *Nossa Senhora da Guia* fishing chapel, which is believed to date back as far as the 10th century! The view over the Atlantic is stunning in any season, but in summer you can take a dip in the sea just next to the chapel on the beach next to the former Forte São João. 📖 *I1*

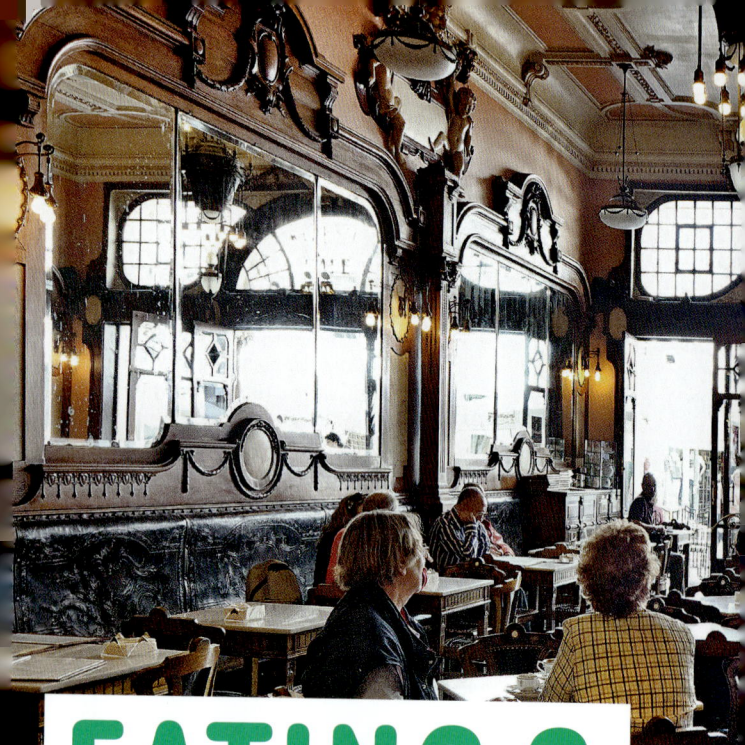

EATING & DRINKING

It's no secret in Portugal that if you're after a good meal, you need to head north. The food is hearty and yet not overly pricey in Porto's classic *tascas*, and there are a few local specialities, including *tripas* (tripe) or *francesinha*.

Dotted among the classic *tascas*, there are now also gourmet restaurants, vegan eateries and plenty of *petiscos*, Porto's take on a tapas bar. Unsurprisingly, prices tend to be on the higher side in tourist hotspots, but the more residential areas still offer plenty of authentic places to eat.

> All the venues in this chapter can be found on the pull-out map 📖

Soak up the Belle Époque atmosphere at Café Majestic

The Portuguese typically enjoy two hot meals a day, but lunch can be just a bowl of hearty soup or a piece of toast topped with melted cheese in a café. Lots of places offer affordable lunch menus. Once it gets to evening, however, the Portuguese properly tuck in, and you might struggle to get a table after 8pm without a reservation. Generally speaking, the local cuisine is pretty meat- and fish-heavy, with vegetables largely taking a back seat – you're most likely to find them in soup.

WHERE TO EAT IN PORTO

Essência

BOAVISTA
Where the locals go to bustling cafés and the Bom Sucesso food market

Casa da Música

Carolina Michaelis

CEDOFEITA

Capela Incomum

Jardins do Palácio de Cristal

RIBEIRA
The Ribeira's alleyways hide tiny bars and restaurants, while the area down by the river pulls in the tourists

300 m / 328 yd

MARCO POLO HIGHLIGHTS

★ CAFÉ MAJESTIC
Travel back to the Belle Époque over a luxury coffee and pastry ➤ p. 64

★ PORTUGUÊS DE GEMA
Excellent Old Town restaurant which employs former homeless people ➤ p. 68

★ A ESCOLA BY THE ARTIST
Students from the hotel school flex their culinary muscles in the in-house bistro ➤ p. 69

★ CAFÉ SANTIAGO
The best place for a proper *francesinha* at the heart of the Baixa ➤ p. 70

★ CAPELA INCOMUM
This chapel-turned-wine bar still has its original altar ➤ p. 71

★ ESSÊNCIA
Top-notch vegetarian restaurant, where you can enjoy a cosy evening on the garden terrace in summer ➤ p. 72

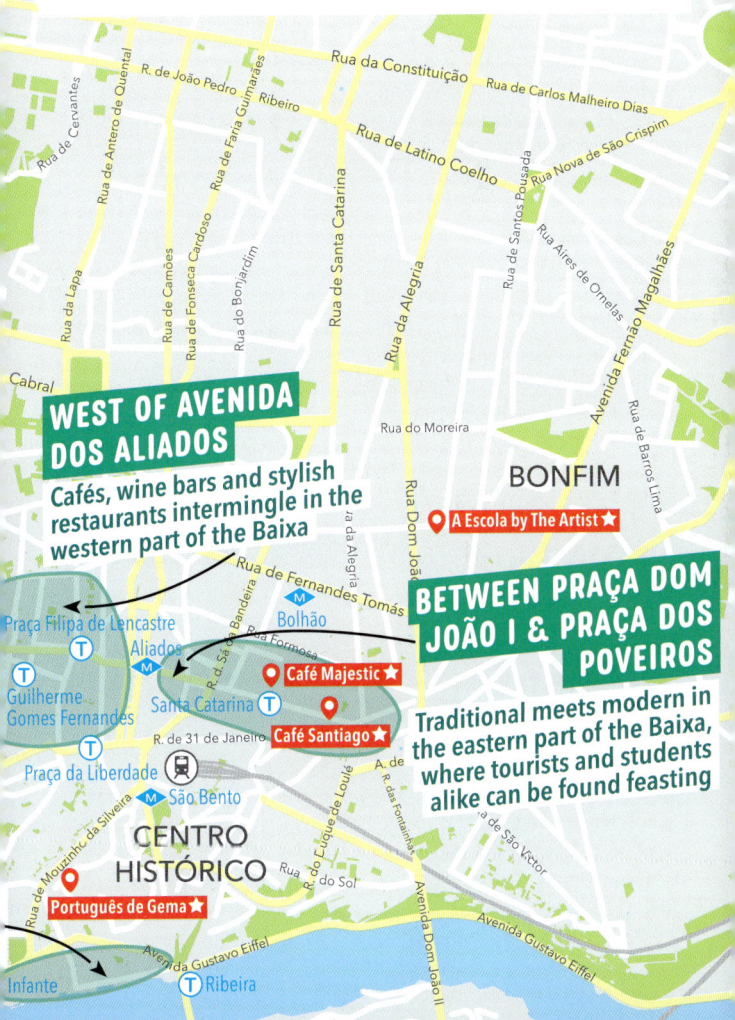

WEST OF AVENIDA DOS ALIADOS
Cafés, wine bars and stylish restaurants intermingle in the western part of the Baixa

BETWEEN PRAÇA DOM JOÃO I & PRAÇA DOS POVEIROS
Traditional meets modern in the eastern part of the Baixa, where tourists and students alike can be found feasting

CAFÉS & ICE-CREAM PARLOURS

CAFÉS & ICE-CREAM PARLOURS

1 CAFÉ ÂNCORA D'OURO (O PIOLHO)
The "Golden Anchor", which has been serving its customers since 1909, earned the nickname "The Louse" thanks to the long-haired students who once frequented the café. Today, the place next to the university is somewhat of a cult spot for staff and students alike. *Mon–Sat 8am–2am | Praça Parada Leitão 45 | tel. 2 22 00 37 49 | FB: Café Piolho | buses Carmo | € | Baixa | ⏍ h6*

2 CERCA VELHA
Former teacher Liliana once dreamed of owning a place like this. And the cosy bistro café down from the cathedral is indeed a dream come true! It's a culinary oasis in the middle of the Old Town, serving snacks and delicious drinks. *Mon, Tue, Thu, Fri 10am–6pm, Sat 10am–7pm, Sun 10am–4.30pm | Largo da Pena Ventosa 23 | tel. 9 14 56 24 99 | FB: Cerca Velha | metro D São Bento | €€ | Old Town | ⏍ h7*

3 DAMA PÉ DE CABRA
The cute little café and shop is the perfect spot for brunch or lunch. Sweet pastries, fresh salads and delicious small dishes made with local ingredients. And no latte (and yes, they're good) is complete here without a heart or smiley face on top. *Tue–Sat 9.30am–3.30pm, Fri/Sat also 7.30–10pm | Passeio de São Lázaro 5 | tel. 2 23 19 67 76 | FB: Dama Pé de Cabra | buses 207, 303, 400 São Lázaro | € | Baixa | ⏍ k6*

4 CAFÉ GUARANY
This cult café takes its name from the South American Guaraní people and has been brightening the city with Brazilian art and coffee since 1933. Plus, there's typical regional (not Brazilian!) food on offer as well as fado in the evening. *Daily 9am–10pm | Avenida dos Aliados 89 | tel. 2 23 32 12 72 | cafeguarany.com | metro D Aliados | €€ | Baixa | ⏍ j6*

5 CAFÉ MAJESTIC ⭐
There's no escaping the city's most famous coffee house! This Belle Époque treasure, complete with sparkling hall of mirrors from 1921, is one of Porto's top attractions. *Mon–Sat 9am–11pm | Rua de Santa Catarina 112 | tel. 2 22 00 38 87 | cafemajestic.com | metro Bolhão | €€ | Baixa | ⏍ j6*

6 DO NORTE CAFÉ
If you enjoy a big breakfast (including lots of fruit) or brunch you will love it here, especially if you're into a bit of ski lodge decor! In the summer, you can sit outside by the natural stone walls. Lunch here is great too. *Daily 8.30am–4pm | Rua do Almada 57/59 | metro D São Bento | € | Baixa | ⏍ h–j6*

7 GELATARIA SINCELO
For over 40 years now, this traditional ice-cream parlour has delighted customers with fresh and fruity ice cream flavours that change by the season. If you're lucky, they might even have their famous port ice cream! *Tue–Thu*

EATING & DRINKING

1–8pm, Fri/Sat 1pm–midnight, Sun 1–10pm | Rua de Ceuta 54 | gelatariasincelo.com | metro D Aliados | *Baixa* | 🕮 h6

8 VIRIATO

INSIDER TIP
A spot of lunch al fresco

When the weather is nice, this café's lovely patio garden is the place to be, sitting among tables filled with students and hospital workers. Lunchtime brings affordable daily specials, with juice and soup available on request. *Mon–Fri 10am–7pm, Sat 11am–6pm | Rua Alberto Aires Gouveia 45 | tel. 9 34 48 41 36 | FB: cafetaria viriato.porto | buses Hospital Santo António | € | Baixa | 🕮 g6*

TRADITIONALLY PORTUGUESE

9 ABADIA

Yes, it's a bit touristy here, but then you do get to dine in a fabulous vaulted restaurant. The atmosphere, as you may have guessed from the name, is reminiscent of an old abbey. Highlights include their delicious *bacalhau* (cod) dishes, but the octopus, ribs and tripe are all also divine. *Closed Mon lunchtime and Sun | Rua de Ateneu Comercial do Porto 22–24 | tel. 2 22 00 87 57 | abadiadoporto. com | metro Bolhão | €€ | Baixa | 🕮 j6*

10 ABRIGO DO PESCADOR

This "safe harbour" is not just for fishermen, but anyone who fancies tucking

Café Guarany has been showcasing Brazilian coffee and art since 1933

TRADITIONALLY PORTUGUESE

Português de Gema

into fresh fish straight from the charcoal grill. While the restaurant itself has been updated, you still have to confront the odd fishing net hanging from the wall. *Closed Tue | Rua Agostinho Albano 102 | tel. 9 35 48 68 20 | buses 902, 903, 907 Chãs | €-€€ | São Pedro da Afurada | C6-7*

11 TABERNA D'AVÓ
This rustic taverna complete with lovingly restored stone walls stays true to its name: "avó" in Portuguese means "grandma". Hearty and welcoming, it is an excellent choice for a proper lunch break. *Closed Mon lunchtime and Sun | Rua de São Bento da Vitória 48 | tel. 2 22 01 21 81 | buses Cordoaria | €€ | Baixa | h6*

12 A COZINHA DO MANEL
The photographs on the wall testify to the Portuguese stars who have dined here at "Manuel's Kitchen", but the real stars are the hearty oven-cooked dishes such as the *vitela* (roast veal) or *cabrito* (goat). *Closed Sun evening and Mon | Rua do Heroísmo 215 | tel. 9 19 78 75 98 | metro Heroísmo | FB: A Cozinha do Manel | €€ | Bonfim | L6*

13 ESCONDIDINHO DO BARREDO
It's the queues that give the game away at this "Little Hideaway" in a Ribeira back alley. The tiny *tasca* might not have a sign on the door or even a name, but busy owner Dona Cremilda hardly needs one! Her father opened the restaurant some 70 years ago and today her daughters rush around helping to serve the hearty *petiscos*, including their delicious fried cod pancakes. *Closed Mon | Rua dos Canastreiros 28 | tel. 2 22 05 72 29 | buses Ribeira | € | Old Town | h-j7*

14 O GAVETO
Matosinhos is all about fish and seafood. You must try their incredible *amêijoas à bulhão pato* (venus clams in a coriander and garlic wine broth). *Closed Tue | Rua Roberto Ivens 826 | tel. 2 29 37 87 96 | restaurante.ogaveto.com | metro A Matosinhos Sul | €€ | Matosinhos | b1*

**INSIDER TIP
Mouth-watering clams**

EATING & DRINKING

Today's specials

Starters

CALDO VERDE
Cabbage soup with potatoes and *chouriço* sausage

SOPA DE LEGUMES
Hearty vegetable soup

GAMBAS COM PIRI-PIRI
Chilli prawns

SALADA DE POLVO
Octopus salad with onions and coriander

Mains

BACALHAU À BRÁS
Cod served with scrambled eggs, onions, thinly sliced fried potatoes, parsley and olives

POLVO À LAGAREIRO
Boiled octopus with garlic and a generous dose of olive oil

SARDINHAS ASSADAS
Fresh sardines cooked on a charcoal grill

FRANCESINHA
Toasted sandwich stuffed with ham, schnitzel and sausage, topped with melted cheese and doused in a spicy red sauce

COZIDO Á PORTUGUESA
A meat stew (beef, pork, chicken and sausage) with potatoes, carrots and green and white cabbage

FRANGO PIRI-PIRI
Grilled chicken marinated in chilli oil

TRIPAS À MODA DO PORTO
Braised tripe with white beans

Desserts

SALADA DE FRUTAS
Fruit salad with apples, citrus fruits, melon and kiwi

PUDIM
Crème caramel

ARROZ DOCE
Portuguese rice pudding

FINE DINING

15 PORTUGUÊS DE GEMA ⭐
This restaurant with its unassuming natural stone walls serves great food and is tucked away down an alley in the Old Town. The eatery is part of a fantastic social project where formerly homeless people prepare delicious traditional regional dishes. We recommend the hearty wild boar and mushrooms or the classic *bacalhau com broa* (cod in a cornbread crumb). *Closed Sun | Rua de Sant'Ana 33 | tel. 2 22 40 00 33 | buses Mouzinho Silveira | FB | €€ | Old Town | ☐ h7*

16 RITO
You should come here if you want to try Porto's traditional tripe or indulge in the excellent northern-style *bacalhau*? Whatever you choose from the menu, which includes, octopus, sea bream or Ibérico pork *(porco preto)*, you won't go away hungry. A half portion *(meia dose)* is more than enough if you're not feeling particularly peckish. *Closed Mon | Rua Antero de Quental 783 | tel. 2 25 40 15 91 | FB: Restaurante Rito Cozunha Regional | metro D Marquês | € | Covelo | ☐ J2*

17 SALTA O MURO
Grill restaurants are ten a penny in Matosinhos, where fresh fish – especially sardines – is grilled right out on the street. But this family restaurant is something special and you might have to wait for a table as they don't take bookings. The restaurant is a mere stone's throw from the harbour, and it doesn't get much fresher than this! *Closed Sun/Mon | Rua Heróis de França 386 | tel. 2 29 38 08 70 | FB: Restaurante Salta O Muro | metro A Brito Capelo | €€ | Matosinhos | ☐ a1*

18 TASCÖ
The bright colours on the plates mirror the boundless enthusiasm of the young team led by chef Rosita. This gastronomic project is stylish, the food is delicious and the atmosphere is friendly. ==The beautifully garnished octopus steals the show.== *Closed at lunchtime | Rua do Almada 151a | tel. 9 24 26 22 33 | otasco.pt | metro D Aliados | €€ | Baixa | ☐ h–j6*

INSIDER TIP
Octopus served bold and bright

FINE DINING

19 ANTIQVVM
This might just be the place for a perfect romantic evening. This restaurant, housed in the Museu Romântico building, has earned a Michelin star for its elegant dishes. Chef Vitor Matos concocts true works of art served with a magnificent view of the garden and river. *Closed Sun/Mon | Rua de Entre-Quintas 220 | tel. 2 26 00 04 45 | antiqvvm.pt | buses Palácio | €€€ | Massarelos | ☐ F6*

20 BBGOURMET MAIORCA
Gourmet cuisine (you must try their tartlets!) at canteen prices. Enjoy colourful and creative dishes from their daily specials or over a coffee in the wonderfully light dining room. *Daily | Rua de António Cardoso 301 | tel. 2 26 09 20 03 | bbgourmet.net | buses 503, 504 Casa de Artes | €–€€ | Arrábida | ☐ D4*

EATING & DRINKING

DOP: a former monastery is the setting for creative takes on traditional cuisine

21 DOP

As if the location – a former Dominican monastery – weren't spectacular enough, head chef Rui Paula conjures up creative menus from traditional recipes. The name DOP – in this case – stands for *Degustar e Ousar no Porto*: taste and be bold in Porto. *Closed Sun/Mon | Largo de São Domingos 18 | tel. 2 22 01 43 13 | doprestaurante.pt | buses Mouzinho Silveira | €€€ |* Old Town *|* h7

22 A ESCOLA BY THE ARTIST ★

So sophisticated are these culinary creations here that you'd never guess your chef was a mere student (albeit from the school of hotel management). And the service is top notch too. What used to be a royal hat factory back in the 19th century was transformed into an art academy in 1927 (hence the name), before the *Escola de Hotelaria e Turismo do Porto* opened a boutique hotel and this renowned bistro restaurant here. *Closed Sun evening | Rua da Firmeza 49 | tel. 2 20 13 27 00 | editoryhotels.com | metro Campo 24 de Agosto | €€ |* Baixa *|* K5

23 MUU STEAKHOUSE

This stylish yet relaxed steak restaurant has just ten tables – and they get snapped up very quickly! If you want to sample what is arguably the best steak in the city, you'll need to book days in advance, but you are guaranteed the best cuts of beef cooked to perfection. If meat isn't your thing, try the *bacalhau* or even the vegan option. *Closed at lunch | Rua do Almada 149a | tel. 9 14 78 40 32 | muusteakhouse.com | metro D Aliados | €€€ |* Baixa *|* h–j6

FRANCESINHA RESTAURANTS

24 PEDRO LEMOS
This beautifully renovated house in Foz do Douro comes with a roof terrace and stunning view of the Douro estuary. Porto's original Michelin-starred chef Pedro Lemos serves seasonal tasting menus. *Closed Sun/Mon | Rua Padre Luís Cabral 974 | tel. 2 20 11 59 86 | pedrolemos.net | tram 1 Passeio Alegre | €€€ | Foz do Douro | c5*

FRANCESINHA RESTAURANTS

Portugal's take on France's *croque monsieur* is called a *francesinha*. More often than not, it's a ham, schnitzel or sausage toasted sandwich topped with heaps of melted cheese and served swimming in a red sauce. Oh, and there are chips! If that's not enough for you, you can always add a fried egg on top. But be warned, you'll be full for the rest of the day!

25 O AFONSO
Celebrity chef Anthony Bourdain raved about his *francesinha* here, which is made with pre-toasted bread. *Closed Mon | Rua da Torrinha 219 | tel. 2 22 00 03 95 | FB: "O Afonso" | bus 602 Torrinha | € | Cedofeita | G5*

26 CERVEJARIA BRASÃO
So which beer goes best with a *francesinha*? Find out at this rustic, down-to-earth bar – the craft beer was developed especially for the dish and has become so popular that it's best to reserve in advance. *Daily | Rua de Ramalho Ortigão 28 | tel. 9 34 15 86 72 | brasao.pt | metro D Aliados | €€ | Baixa | j5–6*

27 CAPA NEGRA II
This is probably the most famous spot for *francesinha* and is definite student territory. The students are especially easy to spot when they wear the traditional *capa negra* or black cape. Of course you can choose the traditional *francesinha* option, but the menu also has plenty of modern takes on the classic. *Daily | Rua do Campo Alegre 191 | tel. 2 26 07 83 80 | capanegra.com | buses Junta Massarelos | € | Massarelos | F5*

28 CAFÉ SANTIAGO ★
Ask Porto's locals and they'll probably tell you that this café, which opened in 1959, serves the best *francesinha* in town. The sausage is fresh from the nearby Mercado do Bolhão and the sauce is just a smidge spicier (and more secret!) than elsewhere. *Closed Sun | Rua de Passos Manuel 226 | tel. 2 22 05 57 97 | cafesantiago.pt | metro Bolhão | € | Baixa | k6*

29 YUKO TAVERN
Decorated like a medieval tavern and with a name that sounds like a sushi restaurant, Yuko Tavern serves predominantly … *francesinhas*. Still, options include cured ham, fresh sausage and a pretty spicy sauce! *Closed Sun | Rua de Costa Cabral 2331 | tel. 2 25 48 22 91 | yuko.com.pt | buses António Coelho | €–€€ | Areosa | I1*

EATING & DRINKING

PETISCOS

30 TASCA DA BADALHOCA 🚩
Sit down with the locals and tuck into huge *sandes de presunto* (ham sandwiches). And if you don't want to leave Porto without trying tripe *petiscos*, this rather out-of-the-way *tasca* is the place to come. *Closed Sat/Sun | Rua Dr. Alberto de Macedo 437 | tel. 2 26 18 53 25 | bus 202 Alberto Macedo | € | Ramalde | ⌑ d3*

31 CAPELA INCOMUM ⭐
The name says it all: "chapel with a difference". Inside this wine bar, you'll find yourself sitting next to the old, intricately carved wooden altar of a former 16th-century chapel. Munch your way through bruschetta and platters of cheese and ham washed down with Portuguese wines. *Closed Sun and at lunchtime | Travessa do Carregal 77 | tel. 9 36 12 90 50 | FB: Capela Incomum | buses and tram Carmo | €–€€ | Baixa | ⌑ h6*

32 JIMÃO TAPAS E VINHOS
Right in the thick of the Ribeira; there's no way you're getting a table here without a reservation – the imaginative tapas really are so good. Ask the friendly and efficient staff to recommend the perfect wine to accompany your *petiscos*. *Closed Sun/Mon | Praça da Ribeira 11–12 | tel. 2 20 92 46 60 | FB: Jimão Tapas e Vinhos | buses Ribeira | €–€€ | Old Town | ⌑ h7*

Café Santiago serves the tastiest francesinha Porto

33 MUSEU D'AVÓ
Given all the memorabilia on the walls, it shouldn't exactly come as a surprise that this bar calls itself "grandma's museum"! Tuck in to hearty *petiscos* and wash them down with the more-than-reasonable house wine. *Closed Sun and at lunchtime | Travessa de Cedofeita 54/56 | tel. 9 33 13 03 82 | FB: Museu d'Avo | metro D Aliados | € | Baixa | ⌑ h5*

VEGETARIAN RESTAURANTS

34 TAPABENTO
You absolutely must try the colourful and creative *petiscos* at this spot just behind São Bento station – if you can find a seat, that is. *Closed Mon/Tue | Rua da Madeira 222 | tel. 9 12 88 12 72 | tapabento.com | metro D São Bento | €€ | Baixa | ⌘ j6*

35 PETISQUEIRA VOLTARIA
With just five bar tables, queues are a common sight outside this mini restaurant – and for good reason: the tapas and small plates are excellent and diverse, and the desserts are out of this world.

> **INSIDER TIP**
> **Sugar rush à la Porto**

The creamy strawberry mousse with port is to die for. Anyway, it's a good thing the place is so small; it has to slot into the smallest street in Porto, after all! *Closed Sun and Wed | Rua Afonso Martins Alho 109 | tel. 2 23 25 65 93 | FB: Petisqueira Voltaria | metro D São Bento | €-€€ | Baixa | ⌘ h-j6*

VEGETARIAN RESTAURANTS

36 EM CARNE VIVA
For a twist on the usual *francesinha* (and probably a welcome change!), here they stuff theirs with aubergine, courgettes, onions or tomatoes!

> **INSIDER TIP**
> **Francesinha goes veggie**

Add in a strong craft beer and even die-hard carnivores won't feel hard done by. Everything else on the menu is just as colourful, creative and delicious. The ambience is both eco-friendly and sophisticated, and in summer you can make yourself at home in the cosy garden. *Closed Sun/Mon and at lunchtime | Avenida da Boavista 868 | tel. 9 32 35 27 22 | emcarneviva.pt | metro Casa da Música | €€ | Boavista | ⌘ E4*

37 ESSÊNCIA ⭐
This chic restaurant dishes up unusual vegetarian creations, as well as a few meat and fish options. It is tucked away in an old villa in a rather elegant residential area from the 1940s. Come summer, you can sit out on the cosy garden terrace. *Closed Sun/Mon | Rua de Pedro Hispano 1190 | tel. 2 28 30 18 13 | essenciavegetariano.pt | buses Casa de Saúde da Boavista | €€ | Boavista | ⌘ F2*

38 SURIBACHI
This paradise for vegetarians and clean eaters has been serving its customers for over 40 years. The macrobiotic buffets change daily, the organic food shop is well stocked and interesting yoga and alternative practitioners feature regularly. *Closed Sun | Rua do Bonfim 134 | tel. 2 25 10 67 00 | suribachi.pt | metro Campo 24 de Agosto | € | Bonfim | ⌘ L6*

39 DA TERRA
If you're tired of fish, there are plenty of fresh vegan/vegetarian options at the buffet here. Other branches have now opened, e.g. in Vila Nova de Gaia or in the Baixa. *Closed Sun evening | Rua Afonso Cordeiro 71 | tel. 2 29 37 08 53 | daterra.pt | metro A Câmara de Matosinhos | € | Matosinhos | ⌘ b1*

EATING & DRINKING

Travel to the mouth of the Douro to try fusion cuisine at Wish Restaurante in Foz Velha

INTERNATIONAL EATERIES

40 BOA-BAO
All the finest delights of Asia – and at reasonable prices. The ambience is stylish here in the nightlife district. *Closed Tue and weekday lunchtimes | Rua da Picaria 61-65 | tel. 9 10 04 30 30 | boabao.pt | metro D Aliados |* €€ | Baixa | m h5-6

41 MUNDO
Are you up for a culinary world tour? Gabriel Silva has drawn inspiration from every continent for his stylish restaurant and its out-of-the-ordinary dishes … accompanied by DJ beats! *Closed at lunchtime | Rua da Picaria 58 | tel. 9 10 74 68 64 | fullest.pt/en/espacos/mundo | metro D Aliados |* €€-€€€ | Baixa | m h5

42 TRATTORIA 179
We've all been there: sometimes you just need pasta or pizza. Try the truffle-mushroom ravioli with parmesan and fresh pesto – it's to die for! *Closed weekday lunchtimes | Rua de Rodrigues Sampaio 179 | tel. 9 64 84 60 87 | trattoria179.pt | metro D Aliados |* €€ | Baixa | m j6

43 WISH RESTAURANTE & SUSHI
Mediterranean meets Japanese here in an exciting culinary explosion. António Vieira creates real taste bombs in an elegant, but not stuffy, ambience on the church square of Foz Velha. *Daily | Largo da Igreja 107 | tel. 9 12 37 53 13 | IG: wish-restaurante | tram 1 Passeio Alegre |* €€-€€€ | Foz do Douro | m c-d5

SHOPPING

The Portuguese love to shop, although less in their city centres and more in large *centros comerciais* on the outskirts. These modern shopping centres come with a *hípermercado*, a huge supermarket, as well as food courts and cinemas – a great way to while away a rainy Saturday. After all, they're nice and dry and air-conditioned, offer underground parking and opening hours that run until 10pm or even midnight … every day of the week!

> All the venues in this chapter can be found on the pull-out map

The magical interior of Livraria Lello wouldn't look out of place at Hogwarts

The Baixa can't quite keep up; here the shops usually shut at 8pm, and smaller shops are closed altogether on Sundays. Still, the pedestrianised streets of the centre are perfect for a stroll, especially Rua de Santa Catarina and Rua das Flores. Alongside all the usual clothing chains, there are still many long-established independent shops and more and more hip boutiques. You'll still meet plenty of Portuguese people here, as you will at the markets, but the average family would probably rather take a trip to the shopping centre when the little ones need new shoes.

WHERE TO SHOP IN PORTO

CEDOFEITA

Craft and creativity, vinyl and vintage in the artists' quarter around Rua de Miguel Bombarda

RUA DAS FLORES

Jewellery, stylish souvenirs and some more unusual pieces fill the shops of this flower-lined pedestrian street

ARRÁBIDA SHOPPING

This, the second-largest shopping centre in the greater Porto area, has over 170 shops, cinemas and restaurants

MARCO POLO HIGHLIGHTS

★ **LIVRARIA LELLO**
The city's most popular bookshop lives up to its far-reaching reputation – and has enchanted the likes of JK Rowling ➤ p. 34, p. 78

★ **THE FEETING ROOM**
Cool kicks, even cooler clothes and freshly roasted coffee. Heaven ➤ p. 79

★ **ARCÁDIA**
Traditional purveyor of all the best things: macarons, pralines, chocolates … ➤ p. 79

★ **MERCADO PORTO BELO**
Alternative flea market for designer and second-hand clothes ➤ p. 83

★ **CC BOMBARDA**
A fresh take on the shopping centres ➤ p. 85

AROUND THE MERCADO DO BOLHÃO
Little grocery stores with big histories surround Porto's largest market hall

RUA DE SANTA CATARINA
Pedestrian zone with its own small shopping centre and all the classic fashion stores

VILA NOVA DE GAIA
Port wine paradise, where you can buy tasty souvenirs direct from the wineries

BOOKS

If you're on the hunt for souvenirs, your best bet is the city centre. You'll find everything you're looking for here, from tiles (you can even paint them yourself!) to culinary treats like cheese, colourful tins of sardines or bottles of port. If you're travelling with hand luggage only, you can easily pick up a bottle of port at the airport, but if you have the luxury of a proper suitcase, the winery shops in Vila Nova de Gaia promise a more authentic experience … and the chance to taste before you buy!

BOOKS

1 FLÂNEUR

This independent bookshop makes for cosy browsing, and they even have a foreign-language section. Don't be shy: Cátia and Arnaldo will be able to recommend just the sort of thing you're looking for. *Tue–Sat 11am–7pm | Rua de Fernandes Costa 88 | flaneur.pt | metro Casa da Música | Boavista | E3*

2 LIVRARIA LELLO ★

Did you know you can offset the €5 you pay to enter Porto's most famous (and undeniably breathtaking) bookshop against the cost of a book? And there are certainly plenty of those to choose from, including some in English. *Daily 9am–7.30pm | Rua das Carmelitas 144 | livrarialello.pt | buses and tram Carmo | Baixa | h6*

CONCEPT STORES & DESIGN

3 Ó! GALERIA

Paradise on Earth for shoppers on the lookout for illustrations, drawings, (personalised) notebooks and pretty much anything else creative. That's hardly surprising, as gallery owner Ema Ribeiro works mainly with young local illustrators and creatives. Try their sister shop, Ó! Cerâmica, a block away, for amazing plates, vases, cereal bowls and the like. You can even watch the artists at work. *Mon–Sat 1–7pm | Rua Miguel Bombarda 61 | ogaleria.com | buses 300, 602 Diogo Brandão | Cedofeita | h5*

INSIDER TIP
Cool ceramics!

4 CRU CREATIVE HUB

If it it's anything to do with art or creativity, it fits the bill at this co-working space. Think clothes, accessories, illustrations and an excellent coffee roaster. *Mon–Fri 9.30am–7.30pm, Sat 10am–7.30pm | Rua do Rosário 211 |*

> **WHERE TO START?**
>
> The **Baixa** is ideal for strolling and shopping. Rua de Santa is your best bet for the fashion chains, Rua de Passos Manuel for shoe shops and Rua das Flores for souvenirs such as painted tiles and culinary gifts. And they are all within a 15-minute walk of each other. If your taste is a little more alternative, head to the bohemian neighbourhood of **Cedofeita** for designer boutiques, vintage and second-hand shops and galleries galore.

78

SHOPPING

crucreativehub.com | buses 300, 602 Miguel Bombarda | *Cedofeita* | g5

5 LOJA
Spread over two floors, Loja sells home furnishings and accessories, including furniture, lamps and books, with an ethos of minimalism and sustainability. The owner, Susana, designed some of the items herself, while other treasures are vintage or created by local artists and designers. *Mon-Sat 2-6pm | Rua de Miguel Bombarda 207 | lojaloja.pt | buses 300, 602 Miguel Bombarda | Cedofeita | g5*

6 CORAÇÃO ALECRIM
This shop, the brainchild of designer Rita, is called "rosemary heart". Rita makes sustainable cotton and linen clothing and also sells furniture, ceramics and plants. The highlight is definitely **Musubu Café** in the pretty green courtyard, which serves the most delicious Japanese rice balls. *Mon-Sat 11am-7pm | Travessa da Cedofeita 28 | coracaoalecrim.com | buses and trams Carmo | Cedofeita | h5*

INSIDER TIP: A taste of Japan

7 THE FEETING ROOM ★
Shopping here is an all-round experience over two floors. As well as exclusive clothes and shoes and stylish accessories for both men and women, this trendy shop offers delicious freshly roasted coffee. Goods include pieces by designers such as Maria Maleta or Nobrand, both from the north of Portugal. *Mon-Sat 10am-8pm, Sun 10am-7pm | Largo dos Lóios 86 | thefeetingroom.com | metro D São Bento | Baixa | h6*

Sweet treats at Arcádia

FOOD & DRINK

8 ARCÁDIA ★
This family business has been creating exquisite chocolates, macarons, pralines and other delicacies for almost 100 years now. Founded in 1933, the original shop boasts shelf after shelf of sweets, as well as a separate space for tastings and events. Old photos on the walls show how the sweets used to be made. The original location is in the Baixa, but there are other branches too now. *Mon-Fri 10am-8pm, Sat 10am-7pm, Sun 11am-7pm | Rua do Almada 63 | arcadia.pt | metro D Aliados | Baixa | h-j6*

FOOD & DRINK

9 CHOCOLATERIA EQUADOR
Temptation alert! The delicious, melt-in-the-mouth chocolates, including some filled with port, are basically tiny works of art. Luckily for chocolate lovers, there are three branches in Porto; this one is near the Mercado Ferreira Borges. *Daily 11am–7pm | Rua de Sousa Viterbo 103 | cacaoequador.pt | bus 403 Ribeira |* Old Town *|* h7

10 GARRAFEIRA DO CARMO
If you are looking for a souvenir of the liquid kind, make sure you visit this bottle shop. Happy customers have been coming here for over 30 years now and you are certain to find exactly what you're looking for in this quaint, well-stocked spot, whether it's wine from the Douro Valley or the Alentejo, fortified Madeira wine, *vinho verde*, or even a liqueur or olive oil. But as you've probably guessed, port is the real star of the show here, including some really old and valuable bottles. Don't forget that you can sample many of the products before you buy. *Mon–Fri 10am–1pm and 2–7pm, Sat 9am–1pm | Rua do Carmo 17-18 | garrafeiracarmo.com | buses and trams Carmo |* Baixa *|* h6

11 MERCEARIA DAS FLORES
Sample traditional Portuguese products such as cheese, sausage, ham, preserves, olive oil and honey before stocking up at this beautiful little grocery store. Most of the products are organic. *Mon–Fri 11.30am–9.30pm, Sat/Sun 12.30–9.30pm | Rua das Flores 110 | merceariadasflores.com | metro D São Bento |* Baixa *|* h7

12 PÉROLA DO BOLHÃO
It's worth visiting the "Pearl of Bolhão" for a photo of the beautifully tiled Art

The Garrafeira do Carmo bottle shop is a must-visit for port drinkers

SHOPPING

Nouveau façade alone. And here you certainly can judge the book by its cover: behind the pretty shopfront is one of the city's oldest and most beautiful grocery stores. Located right next to the Mercado do Bolhão, it has sold spicy cheese from the mountains and Portuguese staples like *chouriço* and *bacalhau* alongside tea, coffee and dried fruit since 1917. *Mon–Fri 9am–7pm, Sat 9am–1pm | Rua Formosa 279 | metro Bolhão | Baixa | j6*

MARKETS

13 FEIRA DE ANTIGUIDADES E VELHARIAS

Heaven on Earth for bargain hunters and hoarders: furniture and coins, porcelain and books, paintings and jewellery and all stretching as far as the eye can see. *Every 3rd Sat of the month 8am–6pm | Praça Francisco Sá Carneiro | metro Estádio do Dragão | Belavista | L–M3*

14 FEIRA DOS PASSARINHOS

Porto's "bird market" does what it says on the tin: join the crowds hunting for a new songbird, or perhaps a cage or useful bird-related accessories. If you're just visiting, you won't be short of things to marvel at. *Sun 7am–1pm | Passeio das Fontaínhas | buses 904, 905 Batalha| Fontaínhas | K7*

15 FEIRA DE PRODUTOS BIOLÓGICOS

This small organic farmers' market in a cul-de-sac near Parque da Cidade blows any supermarket you like out the water. *Sat 8.30am–1.30pm | Beco Carreiras 67 | bus 501 Aldoar Junta Freg. | FB: Feira de Produtos Biológicos Porto | Aldoar | c2*

MARKETS

16 FEIRA DA VANDOMA

This is a proper old school flea market and a veritable treasure trove of second-hand clothes, books, household appliances and all kinds of other odds and ends. *Sat 8am–1pm | Avenida 25 de Abril | buses Av. 25 de Abril | Bonfim | M4*

17 MERCADO MUNICIPAL DA BEIRA RIO

Eighty years after it first opened in 1937, this market hall in the heart of Vila Nova de Gaia, complete with market stalls and places to eat and drink, is a popular destination. Repainted in fresh shades of red, it boasts a compelling cultural programme. Speaking of culture, make sure you take a look at the corner of the building on Rua Dom Afonso III, diagonally behind the market: the giant rabbit made out of rubbish was created by Lisbon street artist Bordalo II. *Daily 11am–10pm, market stalls Mon–Sat 8am–6pm | Avenida Ramos Pinto 148 | mercadobeirario.pt | buses 901, 906 Largo de Aljubarrota | Vila Nova de Gaia | h8*

INSIDER TIP
A rubbish rabbit!

18 MERCADO DO BOLHÃO ★

Ah that unique market scent: flowers with undertones of fish, fruit and hearty veg. This traditional market hall has been given a modern makeover and will soon have all your senses tingling. *Mon–Fri 8am–8pm, Sat 8am–6pm, restaurants open until midnight | Rua Formosa | mercadobolhao.pt | metro Bolhão | Baixa | j5–6*

The Mercado do Bom Sucesso has evolved into a destination food court

SHOPPING

🔟 MERCADO DO BOM SUCESSO

Attempts to transform the "market of good fortune" into a destination have been 100% successful. Originally opened in 1952, today the *mercado* is a temple to the trend. Alongside the usual fruit and vegetables, you'll spot everything from cocktails to seafood, wine to tapas and free shows to gourmet shops. If you're on the hunt for souvenirs of the edible kind, this is a solid bet. *Sun-Thu 8am-11pm, Fri/Sat 8am-midnight | Praça Bom Sucesso 74-90 | mercadobomsucesso.pt | buses Boavista (Bom Sucesso) | Boavista | ▥ F4*

🔢 MERCADO DE MATOSINHOS

You wouldn't struggle to buy a live chicken here – if you so wished – and, of course, there's plenty of fresh fish. But there are also the usual gourmet shops, cafés and snack bars. *Tue-Sat 6.30am-midnight, market stalls Mon 7am-2pm, Tue-Sat 6.30am-6pm, Sat 8.30am-4pm | Rua França Júnior | FB: Mercado Municipal de Matosinhos | metro A Mercado | Matosinhos | ▥ I1*

🔢 MERCADO PORTO BELO ★

This alternative flea market in Porto's bohemian district offers an abundance of chic designer items, colourful pre-loved clothes and regional organic produce. If you love rummaging through unusual, creative jewellery, you'll never want to leave. *Sat 10am-7pm | Praça de Carlos Alberto | FB: Mercado Porto Belo | buses and trams Carmo | Baixa | ▥ h6*

FASHION & VINTAGE

🔢 MON PÈRE VINTAGE

A colourful vintage shop selling unusual pieces at fair prices. There are clothes galore, as well as shoes, sunglasses and accessories. *Mon-Sat 10.30am-7pm | Largo de Alberto Pimentel 38 | IG: monperevintage | metro D Aliados | Cedofeita | ▥ h5*

🔢 QUARTIER LATIN

Head to this row of shops under a modern block of flats near Avenida da Boavista for chic designer clothes, shoes and bags. The catch? They're all second-hand, but then they're all the more affordable for it! *Mon 3-7pm, Tue-Sat 10.30am-1pm and 3-7.30pm | Rua Pedro Homem de Melo 410 | quartierlatin.pt | buses 502, 504 Liceu Garcia Horta | Paços | ▥ d3*

MUSIC

🔢 TUBITEK

A well-stocked record store that still sells music the good old-fashioned way: on new or old, used or still shrink-wrapped CDs and LPs. *Mon-Fri 10am-8pm, Sat 10am-1.30pm and 2.30-7.30pm | Praça de Dom João I 31 | cdgo.com | metro D Aliados | Baixa | ▥ j6*

JEWELLERY

🔢 HOUSE OF FILIGREE

This rather upmarket blend of museum, studio and boutique is dedicated to Portuguese *filigrana*, a delicate goldsmithing art from the

SHOES

north of Portugal. Learn the secrets of the tradition in the museum *(10 euros)*; or attend a workshop (by appointment only) where you can make your very own filigree *(35 euros)*. You can also just pop into the boutique if you simply want to take a look at their jewellery, which for some reason is often heart-shaped. *Tue–Sat 10am–7pm | Rua do Almada 10 | houseoffiligree.pt | metro D São Bento | Baixa | ⌘ j6*

26 LUIZ FERREIRA

This long-established jeweller has sold valuable gifts since 1910. Find it down a side street off the traditional goldsmiths' street Rua das Flores. *Mon–Fri 9.30am–1pm and 3–7pm, Sat 10.30am–1pm | Rua Trindade Coelho 9 | luizferreira.com | metro D São Bento | Baixa | ⌘ j6*

27 WONTHER

Ukrainian-born jewellery designer Olga Kassian champions gender equity and ethical and sustainable materials in her elegant and timeless pieces. See her creations for yourself at *Hotel Torel Palace (Rua de Entreparedes 42 | buses and trams Batalha | Baixa | ⌘ j6). wonther.com*

28 AS 3 JÓIAS

This small shop sells modern handmade jewellery – you can even watch the pieces being made! *Mon–Fri 10am–7pm, Sat 11am–2pm | Rua Santa Teresa 8 | as3joias.com | metro D Aliados | Baixa | ⌘ h6*

SHOES

29 IM STORES

Select brands, expert advice: you're bound to find the shoe for you at one of the four IM Stores shoe and clothing shops in Porto. The branch in Cedofeita is particularly well stocked. *Mon–Fri 9.30am–7pm | Rua de Cedofeita 345 | imstores.pt | bus 301 Torrinha | Cedofeita | ⌘ H5*

SOAP

30 CLAUS PORTO

Claus Porto is *the* name in fine, handmade soaps – and has been for almost 140 years now. Here at the original store, there's also an exhibition detailing the history of their soap empire. *Daily 10am–7pm | Rua das Flores 22 | clausporto.com | buses Mouzinho Silveira | Old Town | ⌘ h7*

SHOPPING MALLS & OUTLET CENTRES

31 ARRÁBIDA SHOPPING

Vila Nova de Gaia's answer to all shopping questions is located on the southern bank of the Douro. The shopping centre is especially popular for eating, as you can enjoy your meal out on a terrace with a view. People are also drawn to the almost 170 different shops, the sheer size of the *hipermercado* and 20 different cinema screens. *Daily 9am–11pm | Praceta de Henrique Moreira 244 | arrabidashopping.com |*

INSIDER TIP Food court with a river view

SHOPPING

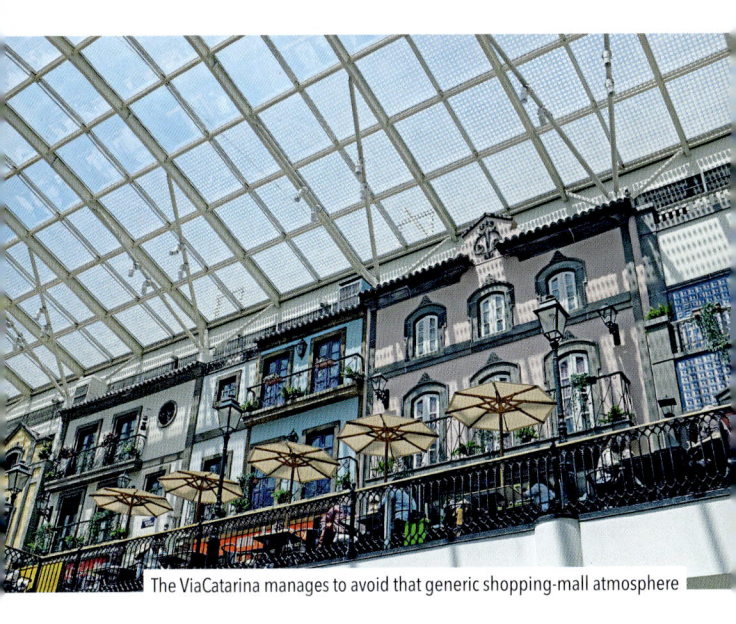

The ViaCatarina manages to avoid that generic shopping-mall atmosphere

buses 902, 907 Arrábida Shopping | Vila Nova de Gaia | E7

32 CC BOMBARDA ★
If you're the sort who'd normally runs for the hills at the dreaded words "shopping centre", you'll love this artistic take on a mall. The alternative shopping centre is full of independent shops that are practically begging you to browse their selection of stunning fashion, jewellery, organic food and plants and more. The green courtyard is the perfect spot for lunch and you never have to wait too long for the next cool event or art exhibition. *Mon-Fri 11am-7pm, Sat 10am-7pm | Rua de Miguel Bombarda 285 | ccbombarda.pt | buses 300, 602 Miguel Bombarda | Cedofeita | g5*

33 VIACATARINA
If you're keen to test the Porto shopping centre experience without leaving the city, this place is for you. Over 70 stores plus restaurants and a supermarket in the heart of the Baixa. *Daily 9am-10pm | Rua de Santa Catarina 312-350 | viacatarina.pt | metro Bolhão | Baixa | j-k6*

34 VILA DO CONDE PORTO FASHION OUTLET
Snap up a bargain on designer clothes, shoes and accessories at this huge outlet centre. Discounts of up to 70 per cent (!) on selected brands will make the metro ride out to Vila do Conde well worthwhile. *Daily 10am-11pm | Avenida Fonte Cova | viladocondefashionoutlet.pt | metro B VC Fashion Outlet-Modivas | Modivas | l1*

NIGHTLIFE

At the weekend, Porto's night owls flock to the Baixa. In places – mostly in the narrow streets around the Rua da Galeria de Paris (which is why the scene has become known as "Galerias") – there's something going on most days of the week thanks to the students and tourists.

The people of Porto often just pop into the pub to grab a drink before heading back outside to relax on the street – weather permitting. Having said that, there are more than enough cafés, wine bars, craft beer pubs and all kinds of other spots where you can

> All the venues in this chapter can be found on the pull-out map 📖

The interior of Galeria de Paris is always entertaining

make yourself comfortable inside, often to the sound of a DJ or live music.

As the night progresses (and almost never before midnight), many people move on to the clubs. The ones in the city centre fill up quite quickly; some more sophisticated clubs have found a home in Boavista and Foz do Douro; larger clubs tend to be on the outskirts.

And then, of course, there are all the concert venues. These come in all shapes and sizes and cater to all tastes. Whatever you're into, you won't get bored in Porto of an evening.

WHERE TO GO OUT IN PORTO

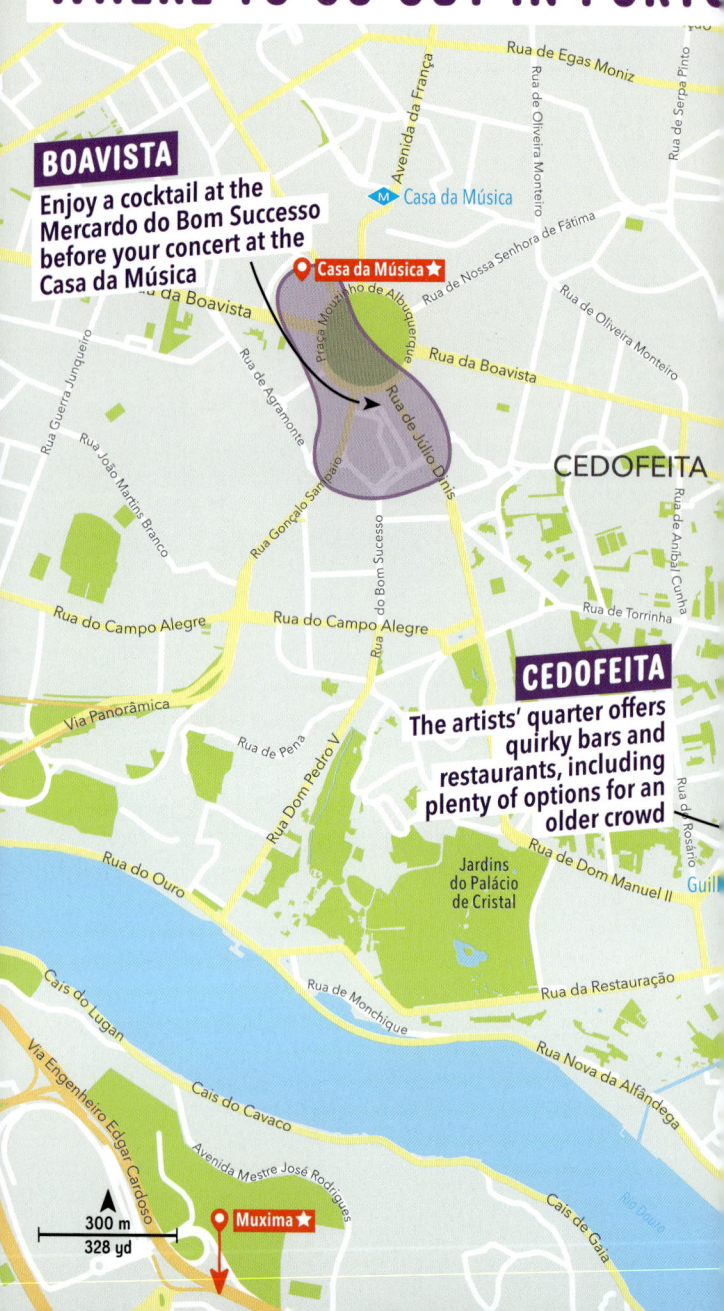

BOAVISTA
Enjoy a cocktail at the Mercardo do Bom Successo before your concert at the Casa da Música

CEDOFEITA
The artists' quarter offers quirky bars and restaurants, including plenty of options for an older crowd

MARCO POLO HIGHLIGHTS

★ CASA DA MÚSICA
A performance at Portugal's futuristic and most illustrious concert hall is an unforgettable experience ➤ p. 47, p. 94

★ FÉ WINE & CLUB
Sophisticated and stylish with excellent wine and a dancefloor ➤ p. 91

★ GALERIA DE PARIS
It's worth visiting for the decorations – made from toys, including Barbies and other dolls – as well as for the chilled atmosphere from morning to night ➤ p. 91

★ LETRARIA
Enjoy a craft beer in the pretty garden ➤ p. 92

★ MUXIMA
Exciting rhythms meet relaxed lounge in Vila Nova de Gaia's coolest dance club ➤ p. 93

★ MAUS HÁBITOS
This cultural centre, with its restaurant, bar, live music and roof terrace, has become something of a second home for many people in Porto ➤ p. 95

BAIXA
Concerts, café-bars, craft beer pubs and cultural centres for all ages

GALERIAS
A party vibe for the students and young tourists who fill the bars and streets here

CENTRO HISTÓRICO

BARS & PUBS

1 BOP CAFÉ
So yes, Bop is a hamburger joint. But the impressive vinyl collection already suggests there's a lot more to the place than just burgers. In the evening, the place transforms into a trendy cocktail bar, and the music's not bad either. And what's really good is that you can always grab a bite to eat – even late at night. *Tue 5pm–midnight, Wed/Thu 10am–11pm, Fri/Sat 10am–1am, Sun 11am–10pm | Rua do Bolhão 124 | bop.pt | metro Bolhão | Baixa | ▢ j5*

2 CAIPICOMPANY
The main attraction here is the heavenly caipirinhas – all different kinds of them (including a tasty alcohol-free version!). This beach bar on Praia do Molhe serves cocktails in a relaxed tropical atmosphere. Delicious salads and snacks are also on offer. *Mon–Thu 10am–10pm, Fri/Sat 10am–midnight, Sun 10am–9pm | Esplanada Praia do Molhe 34 | FB: Caipicompany | bus 500 Molhe | Foz do Douro | ▢ b4*

3 ERA UMA VEZ NO PORTO
"Once upon a time in Porto" ... is a little hidden-away bar – almost like something from a fairytale, you might say! The bar upstairs has a view of the São Bento train station, while downstairs is reserved for dancing, mainly to electronic music. *Tue–Thu 7pm–2am, Fri/Sat 7pm–5am | Rua da Madeira 126 | IG: era_uma_vez_no_porto | metro D São Bento | Baixa | ▢ j6*

4 FABRIK BAR
Industrial style meets industrial music – the name "factory" says it all. This bar

---

WHERE TO START?

Every good night out starts with a good dinner – you'll find plenty of options to the west of Avenida dos Aliados. From there, you're just a stone's throw away from the alleyways of the **Galerias** (▢ j5), where you can visit music cafés and pubs and hang out on the busy streets with a drink. If the clock strikes one and you still want to dance, stay around here or hop in a taxi to one of the cool clubs on the outskirts of the city.

NIGHTLIFE

On warm evenings, the streets of Galerias are the place to be

in the middle of the nightlife district is LGBTQ+-friendly and is a cracking place to dance. *Tue/Wed 6pm–2am, Thu 6pm–3am, Fri/Sat 6pm–4am | Rua da Galeria de Paris 109 | FB: Fabrik Bar | buses and trams Carmo | Baixa | h6*

5 FÉ WINE & CLUB ⭐

This modern wine bar brings elegance and more than a touch of the colour red to Porto's nightlife district. Prices aren't the lowest, but the cocktails are pretty elaborate! The music tends towards chilled jazz and there's a dance floor for if you feel inclined. *Mon/Tue 6pm–midnight, Wed/Thu 6pm–2am, Fri/Sat 6pm–4am | Praça Dona Filipa de Lencastre 1 | feporto.pt | metro D Aliados | Baixa | h–j6*

6 FERRO BAR

Where there's a railway, there's a … "railway bar"? This alternative bar has strong garage vibes but there's also a terrace with the odd jam session now and then. Snack food is available in case you get peckish. *Tue–Thu 7pm–5am, Fri/Sat 6pm–5am, Sun 2pm–5am | Rua da Madeira 84 | FB: Ferro Bar | metro D São Bento | Baixa | j6*

7 GALERIA DE PARIS ⭐

Café/restaurant by day, club by night. So, where you enjoyed breakfast in the morning, you can nibble on a snack at lunchtime *(€–€€)*, listen to *fado* then sip a cocktail in the evening, and finally dance the night away. Then repeat – you could almost move in here! However long you stay, make

BARS & PUBS

sure you take a look at the toy dolls and other knick-knacks that line the walls of this multitasking bar. *Mon 9am–7pm, Tue–Thu 9am–3am, Fri/Sat 9am–4am | Rua da Galeria de Paris 56 | FB: Galeria de Paris | buses and trams Carmo | Baixa | ⌘ h6*

8 LETRARIA ⭐

The menu features some 100 different beer creations – hence the subtitle "Craft Beer Garden". The pretty garden is a real hit and is the perfect place to sit for a while in the summer.

INSIDER TIP Enjoy a beer in a green oasis

Well, you've got a lot of beer to get through, after all! *Sun–Thu 4pm–midnight, Fri 5pm–1am, Sat 12.30pm–2am | Rua da Alegria 101 | cervejaletra.pt | metro Bolhão | Baixa | ⌘ k6*

The Royal Cocktail Club

9 ONTOP

Roof-top bars are starting to become synonymous with the word "hotel", and the HF Ipanema Park is no exception. The view from the 15th floor is exceptional, especially looking out towards the Douro estuary. The glass walls keep the brisk Atlantic winds off, so you can sip your cocktail in peace. *Daily in good weather 8pm–1am | Rua de Serralves 124 | hfhotels.com | buses Lordelo | Lordelo de Ouro | ⌘ C4*

10 PIPA VELHA

This long-established bar attracts a very mixed crowd. Posters from its early days – over 40 years ago – still hang on the walls. *Daily 5pm–4am | Rua das Oliveiras 75 | FB: Pipa Velha | metro D Aliados | Baixa | ⌘ h5*

11 PIXOTE KARAOKE BAR

People have been singing their hearts out in this legendary karaoke bar since 1986 … some better than others! But don't panic, you can choose from plenty of international favourites alongside the Portuguese hits. *Daily 11pm–4am | Rua do Campo Alegre 241 | FB: Pixote Karaoke Bar Porto | buses Junta Massarelos | Massarelos | ⌘ F5*

12 GUINDALENSE F. C.

While the Guindalense Futebol Clube no longer operates a football pitch, the venue (and the bar) remains. The prices are unbeatable and so is the view.

INSIDER TIP FC club venue with a view

Mon–Fri noon–11pm, Sat 1pm–midnight | Escadas dos Guindais 43 |

NIGHTLIFE

FB: Guindalense FC | buses Elevador Guindais | Ribeira | 📖 j7

13 THE ROYAL COCKTAIL CLUB
If you prefer to drink in style, you won't be disappointed here. The cocktails – good luck sticking to just one – are sophisticated, delicious and fruity.

> **INSIDER TIP**
> **Mixology heaven**
> The experienced mixologists here have a signature cocktail or two up their sleeves.

What's more, the music is kept low so you can have a proper chinwag. *Sun-Thu 7pm-2am, Fri/Sat 7pm-4am | Rua da Fábrica 105 | FB: The Royal Cocktail Club | metro D Aliados | Baixa | 📖 h6*

14 TABERNA ADUELA
This bar is loved by locals and tourists alike. If the weather's good, you can draw up a seat on the small, triangular plaza under the olive trees and soak up the atmosphere. Make sure you try their delicious small plates to go with your wine, sangria or beer. *Tue-Sat 10am-2am, Sun noon-midnight, Mon 6pm-2am | Rua das Oliveiras 36 | FB: Aduela taberna-bar | buses & trams Carmo | Baixa | 📖 h6*

CLUBS

15 CAFÉ AU LAIT
There's definitely more going on than milky coffee here! Café au Lait is a cool night bar with groovy music, a chilled atmosphere and no hassle from the bouncers. At the weekend there is a varied guest DJ set. *Mon-Sat 3pm-4am | Rua da Galeria de Paris 46 | FB: Café au Lait | buses and trams Carmo | Baixa | 📖 h6*

16 BOÎTE
This might just be the trendiest nightclub in the city, with funky interior design to match. The elaborate light show will have you feeling like you're dancing in outer space. The music is mostly dance, hip hop and pop. As if the place weren't cool enough already, there's also a chic wine bar serving sophisticated cocktails. *Mon, Wed, Fri, Sat 11pm-6am | Rua de Passos Manuel 131 | IG: boiteporto | metro Bolhão | Baixa | 📖 j6*

17 ESKADA
As befits the stylish vibes, the clientele here is chic and certainly on the younger side. The music is mostly pop or whatever is in the charts. *Mon and Wed-Sat midnight-6am | Rua da Alegria 611 | FB: Eskada Porto | metro D Marquês | Bonfim | 📖 K4*

18 INDÚSTRIA
While you'll usually hear electronic music in this popular club at Foz do Douro's Praia do Molhe, there are also alternative sounds from time to time, and guest DJs make a regular appearance. The sound is great, but it can get quite hot and sweaty on the dancefloor. *Usually Fri/Sat midnight-6am | Avenida do Brasil 843 | buses 1M, 500 Molhe | Foz do Douro | 📖 b4*

19 MUXIMA ⭐
Vila Nova de Gaia has its fair share of outdoor celebrations. The wooden dancefloor here loves to transport its

93

CONCERTS & THEATRE

Casa da Música

20 TENDINHA DOS CLÉRIGOS
The city's revellers usually warm up in the Galerias, so it's hardly surprising that this mini club right in the heart of the nightlife district fills up as soon as the night gets going. Rock is the name of the game here: the music is mainly classics from the 1970s to the 90s. *Fri/Sat midnight–6am | Rua Conde de Vizela 80 | tendinhadosclerigos.com | metro D Aliados | Baixa | h6*

21 ZOOM
Porto's most famous gay club is located in an old warehouse. A LGBTQ+-friendly space to dance to pop and house music at weekends. Well-built go-go dancers add that *je ne sais quoi*. *Fri/Sat 12.30–6am | Rua de Passos Manuel 40 | zoomporto.wixsite.com/zoomporto | metro D Aliados | Baixa | j6*

CONCERTS & THEATRE

22 CASA DA MÚSICA ★
The gold-leaf-clad main hall, Sala Suggia, programmes mostly (but not only) classical music, while the smaller halls host more experimental performances. Whichever you choose, a concert in this futuristic concert building and first-class music venue is a sure highlight of any trip to Porto. If you're under 25, you get 50 per cent off – same goes for music students and teachers. *Avenida da Boavista 604 | casadamusica.com | metro Casa da Música | Boavista | F4*

guests to other parts of the world: Tuesday is African night with Kizomba & Co., while Fridays and Saturdays are for Afro and Latino rhythms. Up on stage, professional dancers get the audience moving. If you know all the dancing is going to leave you thirsty, you can reserve a table online for a cocktail and a snack. *Tue, Fri, Sat 11pm–4am | Rua Maurício Lourenço de Oliveira 206 | muximabar.com | taxi | Vila Nova de Gaia | l1*

INSIDER TIP Learn from the best

INSIDER TIP Half-price concerts

NIGHTLIFE

23 CASA DA MARIQUINHAS

Fado is not just reserved for Lisbon or Coimbra; there's plenty in Porto too. *Fadistas* have sung their melancholy tunes to the sounds of a viola and a Portuguese guitar in this traditional restaurant since 1968 – don't worry, not all the songs are sad. Dishes are traditional and the wine is good (minimum spend 45 euros). Reservations essential! *Mon–Sat from 8pm | Rua de São Sebastião 25 | tel. 9 15 61 3 8 77 | casadamariquinhas.pt | buses Mouzinho Silveira | Old Town | ⌑ h–j7*

24 COLISEU DO PORTO

This Art Deco building dates back to 1941 and is Porto's top address for pop and rock concerts. As well as all the national stars, international bands perform from time to time. *Rua de Passos Manuel 137 | coliseu.pt | metro Bolhão | Baixa | ⌑ j–k6*

25 HARD CLUB

The former Mercado Ferreira Borges market hall dates back to 1885 and today hosts rock concerts and club events. Before the night gets underway, grab a bite to eat in the trendy restaurant *(daily | €€)* on the upper floor. *Praça do Infante Dom Henrique | hardclubporto.com | buses Ribeira | Old Town | ⌑ h7*

26 TEATRO MUNICIPAL RIVOLI

Porto's city theatre is housed in a magnificent building dating from 1913, right in the middle of the Baixa. The theatre programme is varied. *Praça Dom João I | teatromunicipaldoporto. pt | metro D Aliados | Baixa | ⌑ j6*

CULTURAL CENTRES

27 CASA ALLEN & CASA DAS ARTES

This complex may as well be called the "House of Culture", because there is plenty of it here! The beautiful *Casa Allen*, which dates back to the late 1920s, and especially the garden *Casa das Artes*, which was built by Eduardo Souto de Moura, host readings, workshops and other cultural events. Thursdays at 9.30pm and Saturdays at 6pm are for film screenings. All genres of old or independent films are shown – in the original language, of course! *Rua Ruben A 210 | casadasartes.gov.pt | buses 503, 504 Casa das Artes | Arrábida | ⌑ D4*

INSIDER TIP — The art of cinema in the house of art

28 MAUS HÁBITOS ★

This legendary cultural centre sits above a car park in the heart of the Baixa and bears the curious name "Bad Habits". Its mix of affordable restaurant, live music and cocktail bar, and exciting art and concert programme has seen it become something close to a second home to many a local. On sunny days, and warm nights, the blue and lovingly landscaped roof terrace is a perfect spot for hanging out. *Mon 6pm–midnight, Tue/Wed noon–midnight, Thu noon–2am, Fri/Sat noon–6am | Rua de Passos Manuel 178 | maushabitos.com | metro Bolhão | Baixa | ⌑ j6*

ACTIVE & RELAXED

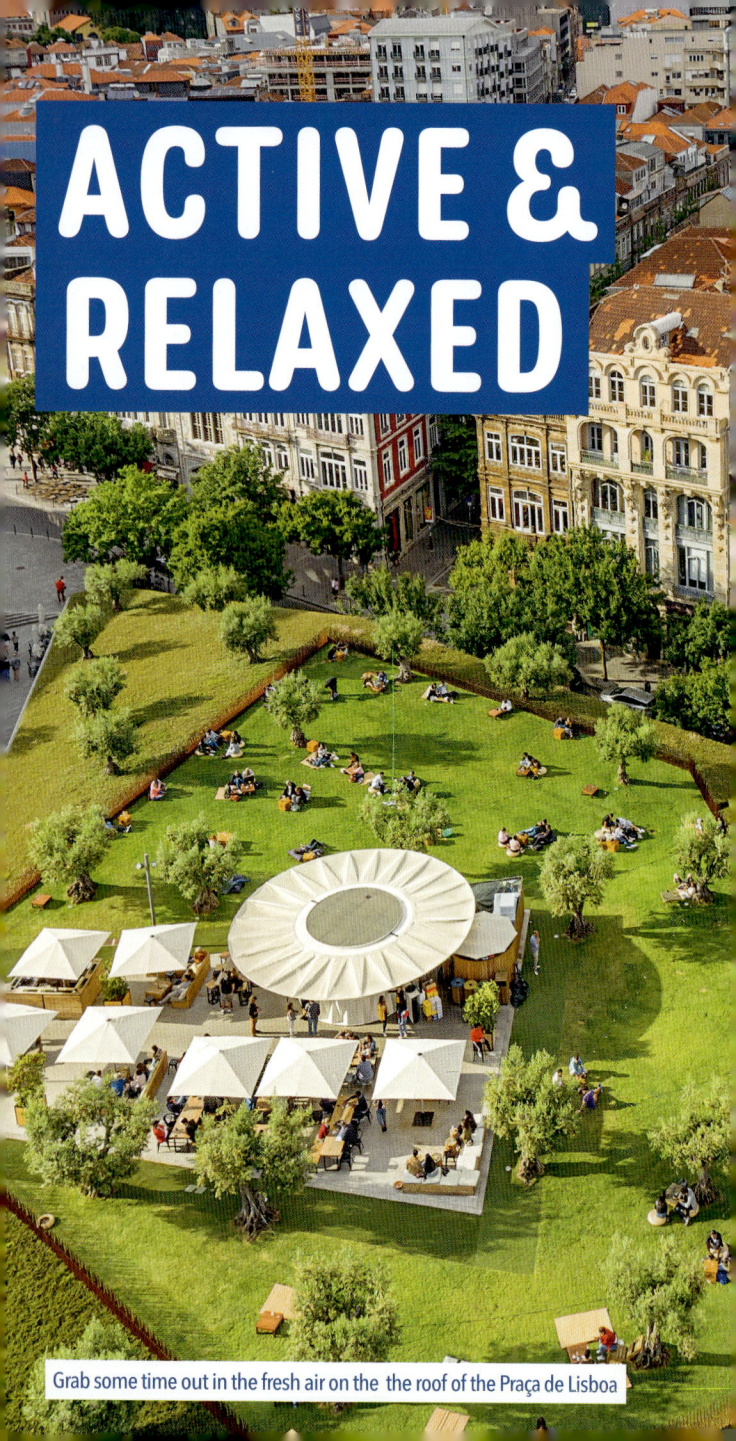

Grab some time out in the fresh air on the the roof of the Praça de Lisboa

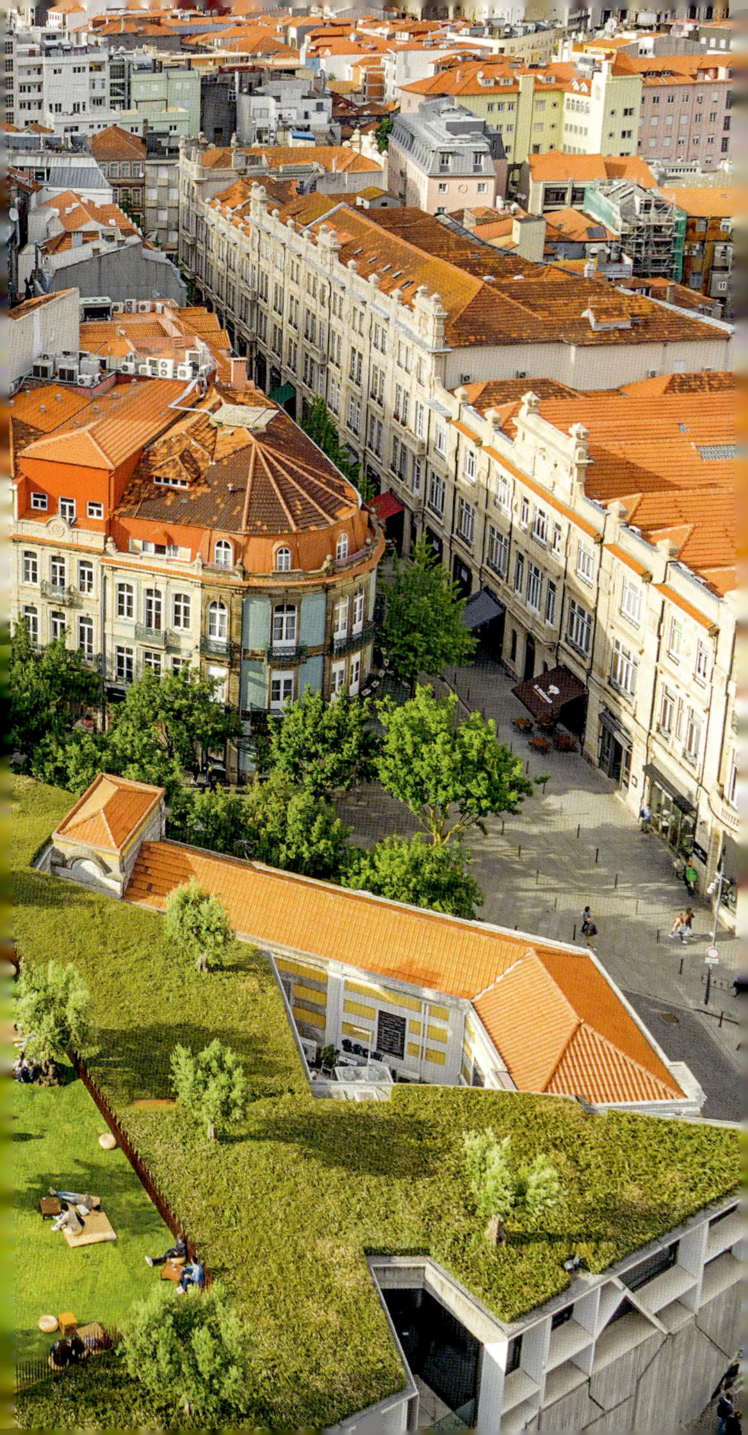

SPORT & WELLNESS

BRIDGE CLIMBING
Scale the immense concrete arch of the Ponte da Arrábida (by appointment)! Don't worry, you are safely roped up and led by an experienced guide from *Porto Bridge Climb (from 16 euros/person | Rua do Ouro 680 | tel. 9 29 20 71 17 | portobridgeclimb. com)*. And, 65m above the river, the view is out of this world!

CYCLING
If you're not averse to the odd incline, you can get around Porto by bike – although be warned that the cycle-path network is still in its infancy. The most beautiful (and flattest!) routes are along the banks of the Douro and the Atlantic. Rent a decent bike from e.g. *Velurb (Mon–Fri 9.30am–1pm and 2.30–7pm, Sat 9.30am–1pm | from 12 euros/day | Rua Fernandes Tomás 207 | tel. 9 18 50 61 33)*.

FOOTBALL
A visit to an FC Porto home game at the *Estádio do Dragão* is a must for die-hard football fans. Online tickets start at 22 euros *(fcporto.pt)*. But the Boavista Futebol Clube also plays in the premier league and usually gives the bigger clubs a hard time. The atmosphere is always electric at the local derby! Their home ground is the *Estádio do Bessa (Rua O Primeiro do Janeiro | boavistafc.pt)*. Tickets available online at: *smartfan.tickets/boavistafc*.

INSIDER TIP: Root for the underdog

GOLF
Portugal as a country certainly has no shortage of golf courses. One course with a very pleasant restaurant is the *Quinta do Fojo (green fee for 18 holes is 23 euros | Rua Nova do Fojo 238 | golfojo.com)* in the Canidelo district of Vila Nova de Gaia.

Take the metro from the city to the surf at Praia de Matosinhos

JOGGING

There are plenty of stunning jogging trails, including the Parque da Cidade, along the Douro or along the Atlantic coast, all of which are popular with locals. The south bank of the Douro has a particularly nice section: behind the Burmester port cellar, a narrow road (Rua Cabo Simão) leads along the hillside; from the Ponte do Infante it becomes a beautiful path and later even turns into a metal walkway directly alongside the water. Behind the Areinho river beach, it passes under the Ponte do Freixo and then it's back along the same route.

**INSIDER TIP
Upstream away from the cars**

WATERSPORTS

Porto's surfers flock to Matosinhos beach. Take a course or rent equipment from e.g. *Onda Pura (4 lessons for 80 euros | Praia de Matosinhos | ondapura.com)* if you want to learn to surf or test the waves of the Atlantic for yourself. The *Paddling Center (paddlingcenter.pt)* in the marina of São Pedro da Afurada is the place to go for kayaking or SUP lessons, and there are also tours along the Douro.

WELLNESS

If you're hoping to destress in Porto, your best bet is a hotel with spa. Most allow non-residents to use their facilities, including pools, jacuzzis and saunas – for example the *Sheraton (50 euros/day | Rua Tenente Valadim 146 | thespaporto.com)*. Book a massage and use of the spa is included in the price!

FESTIVALS & EVENTS

FEBRUARY
Essência do Vinho *(essenciadovinho porto.com)*: International fair for winemakers, wine merchants and plain old lovers of wine at the Palácio da Bolsa.
Fantasporto *(fantasporto.com)*: International film festival at the Batalha Centro de Cinema.

MARCH
Comic Con *(evento.comic-con-portugal.com)*: Portugal's biggest pop-culture festival draws comic and gaming fans to the Exponor in Matosinhos.

APRIL
Festival Dias de Dança *(festivalddd.com)*: Contemporary dance events and workshops at various locations over the course of several weeks.

MAY
Queima das Fitas *(queima.fap.pt)*: This student festival features various parades through the city and concerts in Parque da Cidade.

MAY/JUNE
Serralves em Festa *(serralves.pt)*: A diverse, 50-hour non-stop culutral event in Serralves Park.
Festas do Senhor de Matosinhos *(leca-palmeira.com)*: A three-week festival with processions, concerts, fireworks and a fair to celebrate the city's patron saint.

JUNE
Primavera Sound *(primaverasound.com)*: An alternative-inspired international rock and pop festival in Parque da Cidade.
Festas da Cidade: A whole month of concerts, cultural and sporting events. The highlight is the *Noite de São João* (23/24 June) when fireworks light up the Douro.

Everyone takes to the streets to celebrate the Noite de São João

Festa de São Pedro de Afurada: This traditional saint's day festival for St Peter takes place around the 29 June with a large procession.

JULY/AUGUST
MEO Marés Vivas *(maresvivas.meo.pt)*: This rock festival in Vila Nova de Gaia boasts a high-profile line-up and Atlantic view.
Jazz no Parque *(serralves.pt)*: Jazz festival in Serralves park.
Porto Pianofest *(portopianofest.com)*: Renowned pianists take to the stage in venues such as the Casa da Música, the university, the World of Wine or the Palácio da Bolsa.

SEPTEMBER
Meia Maratona do Porto *(meiamaratonadoporto.com)*: Half marathon.
Feira do Livro *(feiradolivro.porto.pt)*: Porto's book fair is held in the Jardins do Palácio de Cristal.

Gaia World Music *(cm-gaia.pt/pt/eventos)*: Music from around the world – and free entry! – in Jardim do Morro, at Mosteiro da Serra do Pilar and in the Corpus Christi Monastery.

OCTOBER
Festival International de Marionetas do Porto *(fimp.pt)*: Puppet theatre festival across several venues.
Portugal Fashion *(portugalfashion.com)*: Fashion festival in the Alfândega Nova.

NOVEMBER
Misty-Fest *(misty-fest.com)*: High-profile music festival held across several Portuguese cities.
Porto Marathon *(porto-marathon.com)*: A 42.2km riverbank route.

DECEMBER
New Year's Eve: Concerts and fireworks on Avenida dos Aliados.

SLEEP WELL

NIGHT AT THE MUSEUM
The lavishly renovated bourgeois palace *Espaço Palmeiras (5 suites | Travessa de São Carlos 7 | tel. 9 14 86 59 94 | espacopalmeiras.pt | metro Trindade | €€€ | Baixa | H5)* is not called the *Palace Museum* for nothing: all the stucco, wall paintings and furniture from the late 19th century is enough to make you feel like a member of Porto's bourgeoisie.

CURTAIN UP!
It's true, the *Porto Bay Teatro (74 rooms. | Rua Sá da Bandeira 84 | tel. 2 20 40 96 20 | portobay.com | metro D São Bento | €€€ | Baixa | j6)* isn't actually a real theatre, but it sure does look like one! A prop stand here, a spotlight there ... The dimmed lights alone will have you thinking the curtain is about to come up. There really was a theatre here once upon a time: the Teatro Baquet was inaugurated in 1859 but tragically burnt down in 1888. Fast forward 120 years and this stylishly dark theatre hotel opened on the same site.

DODGING DODGEMS
The sweeping Art Deco staircase exudes nostalgic glamour in this hotel from 1958. Yet the reception of the *Pão de Açucar (61 rooms | Rua do Almada 262 | tel. 2 22 00 24 25 | paodeacucarhotel.pt | metro D Aliados | € | Baixa | j6)* is a slightly more chaotic experience, with old microphones and chewing gum machines littering the area. To get to your room, you'll have to navigate past dodgems and petrol pumps from the 1970s. This place certainly isn't for the faint-hearted: there are probably around 500 items of vintage paraphernalia in total. Still, the price is fair for the central location and the rooms are thankfully kept simple.

Room with a view at The Yeatman

A HAVEN FOR ART LOVERS & CREATIVES

If art is your thing, the location just couldn't be better. This hostel is located right at the heart of Porto's art district, a stone's throw from the trendiest vintage shops and nightlife spots. Back in 2011, a family took on the building, which dates back to 1906, determined to renovate it sustainably. And they succeeded! Today, the *Gallery Hostel (41 beds | Rua de Miguel Bombarda 222 | tel. 2 24 96 43 13 | gallery-hostel.com | buses and trams Carmo | € | Cedofeita | g-h5)* is an artistic, family-friendly hostel with its very own gallery. It also hosts bi-monthly art exhibitions and exciting (art) events, and guests are welcome to join in the fun. There are dormitory-style rooms or the garden area offers two spacious twins and a triple room.

ENJOY WINE IN STYLE

The luxury accommodation in *The Yeatman (109 rooms | Rua do Choupelo | tel. 2 20 13 31 00 | the-yeatman-hotel.com | metro D General Torres | €€€ | Vila Nova de Gaia | l1)* is all about wine. This is not surprising given its location high above the port cellars of Vila Nova de Gaia, which also means it enjoys the most incredible view of Porto. Those with enough cash in their pockets can even sleep in a bed made out of wine barrels in the presidential suite. The elegant hotel restaurant (which of course serves all the best Portuguese wines) has two Michelin stars to its name, and you can relax and unwind with a vinotherapy treatment in the magnificent spa.

DISCOVERY TOURS

Do you want to get under the skin of the city? Then these discovery tours provide the perfect guide. They include advice on which sights to visit, tips on where to stop for that perfect holiday snap, a choice of the best places to eat and drink and suggestions for fun activities.

The glorious central hall of Porto's Estação de São Bento

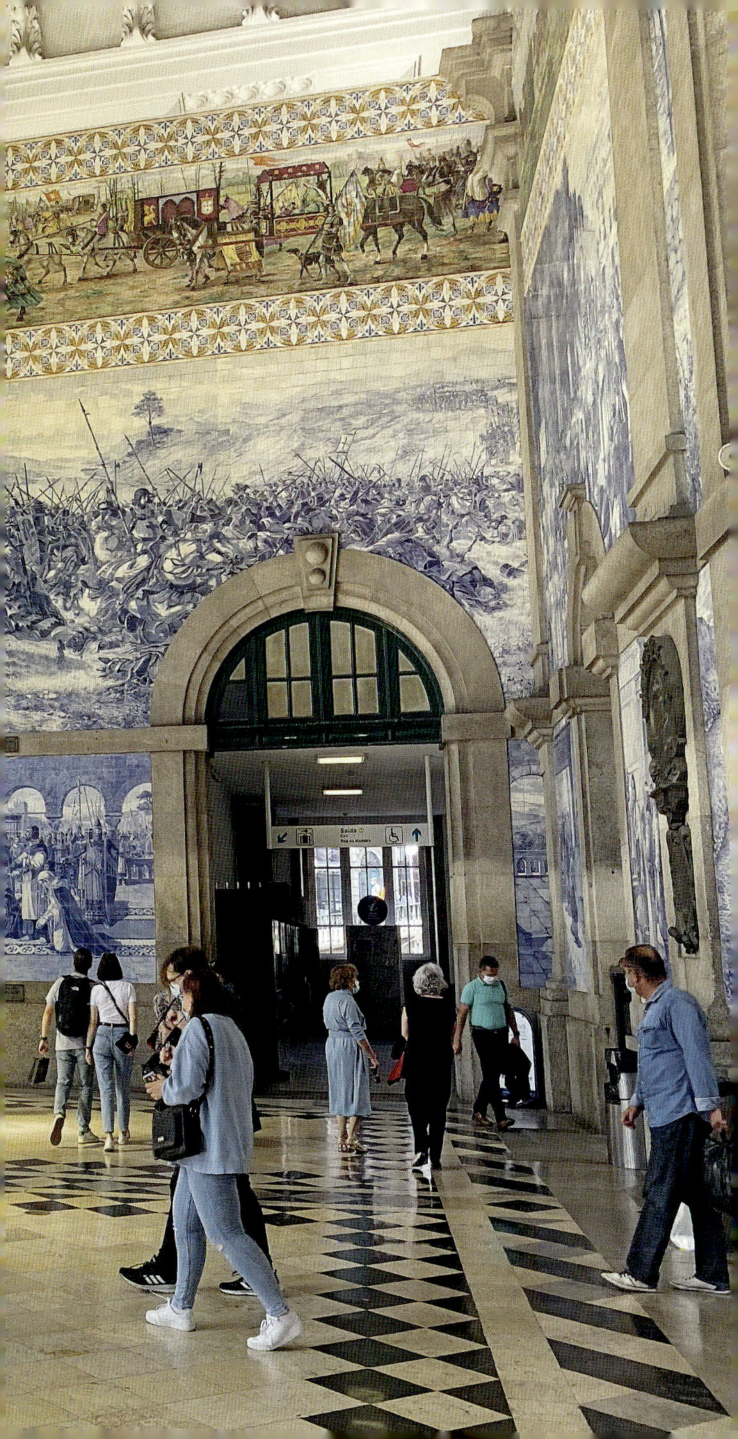
Saída

DISCOVERY TOURS
AN OVERVIEW

Santa Cruz do Bispo

Guifões

Leça da Palmeira

Matosinhos

Aldoar

Parque da Cidade

Nevogilde

Foz do Douro

Lordelo do Ouro

Matosinhos by bike

OCEANO ATLÂNTICO

Rio Douro

1 km
0.62 mi

Gueifães
Leça do Balio
Custóias
São Mamede de Infesta
Pedrouços
Senhora da Hora
Paranhos
Ramalde
Porto
Cedofeita
Bonfim
Campanhã
São Pedro da Afurada
Vila Nova de Gaia
Santa Marinha
Oliveira do Douro
Rio Leça
Autoestrada de Trás-os-Montes e Alto Douro
A4
A3
A20
A1
A44
IC23
Via Norte
Rua de Gondivai
Rua de Recarei
R. de Catassol
Rua de Santana
A. Doutor Germano Vieira
R. da Vessada
R. de Agra
R. M. Gonçalves Lage
Autoestrada de Trás-os-Montes e Alto Douro
A. de Entre-Douro-e-Minho
Rua de Henrique Bravo
Rua 5 de Outubro
R. de Silva Brinco
Rua Dom Afonso Henriques
Rua Nova do Seixo
Estrada Interior da Circunvalação
R. do Monte
Rua Dom João Coutinho
Via de Cintura Interna
Circular Regional Interior do Porto
Rua de Costa Cabral
Avenida de Fernão Magalhães
Circular Regional Interior do Porto
Rua da Constituição
R. de Pedro Hispano
A. de França
Guimarães
Rua da Alegria
Rua da Boavista
Avenida 25 de Abril
Rua do Campo Alegre
Rua de Júlio Dinis
Autoestrada do Litoral Norte
Rua Dom João IV
Rua do Bonfim
R. de Sá da Bandeira
R. do Heroísmo
R. Nova da Alfândega
Avenida Gustavo Eiffel
Avenida de Paiva Couceiro
Ponte do Freixo
Via de Cintura Interna
Via Engenheiro Edgar Cardoso
Avenida da República
Avenida Dom João II
Porto's street art
Porto at a glance
Porto's lesser-known east side
1
3
4

① PORTO AT A GLANCE

- ➤ Wander through the Baixa and Ribeira to Vila Nova de Gaia
- ➤ Enjoy breathtaking views of the Douro and a boat trip to boot
- ➤ Travel above the port cellars in a cable car

📍	Avenida dos Aliados	🚩	Mosteiro da Serra do Pilar
→	approx. 6 km	🚶	1 day (total walking time approx. 1½ hrs)

ℹ️ During peak season, we recommend booking the 6-bridge boat tour in advance *(daily 10am–6pm | 18 euros)*, e.g. through Tomáz do Douro *(tomazdodouro.pt)*.

❶ Avenida dos Aliados

❷ Igreja do Carmo

❸ Livraria Lello

❹ Torre dos Clérigos

❺ Estação de São Bento

❻ Mercado do Bolhão

PORTO'S HIGHLIGHTS IN THE BAIXA!

Start where Porto's heart beats loudest (not to mention the current din from ongoing metro construction) on the magnificent ❶ **Avenida dos Aliados** ➤ **p. 30**. From here, *take Rua da Fábrica, passing the Galerias nightlife district, to end up on Praça de Carlos Alberto*. You won't have long to wait before you see the blue and white *azulejo*-clad side façade of the ❷ **Igreja do Carmo** ➤ **p. 35**. Once you've seen inside, it'll be time to discover a whole new world *at the other end of the square in front of the university*: the neo-Gothic façade of ❸ **Livraria Lello** ➤ **p. 34 and 78** hides one of the most beautiful (and most crowded!) bookshops in the world. *Cross the Praça de Lisboa (this car park roof has been transformed into a green space)* to reach Porto's most significant landmark: the ❹ **Torre dos Clérigos** ➤ **p. 34**. Climb the church tower for a view of almost the entire city. Make sure to have a look inside the Baroque church itself too.

Next, head down Rua dos Clérigos. At Praça da Liberdade you'll once again see Avenida dos Aliados in all its glory. Not much further and it's time to admire the stories written in the *azulejos* of the station concourse of ❺ **Estação de São Bento** ➤ **p. 33**. *Walk along the shopping street Rua Sá da Bandeira* to reach the freshly renovated ❻ **Mercado do Bolhão** ➤ **p. 31**

DISCOVERY TOURS

and p. 82: the wrought-iron market hall is a feast for all the senses. *Exit at the upper end,* and you will reach the blue- and white-tiled ❼ **Capela das Almas de Santa Catarina**; *stroll down the pedestrianised Rua de Santa Catarina to Praça da Batalha.* The ❽ **Igreja de Santo Ildefonso** ➤ p. 32 is another magnificent example of *azulejo* design.

❼ Capela das Almas de Santa Catarina

❽ Igreja de Santo Ildefonso

TIME FOR LUNCH

Tucked away at the southern end of Praça da Batalha, the traditional ❾ **Cervejaria Gazela** *(closed Sun | Rua de Entreparedes 8–10 | tel. 2 21 12 49 81 | cervejaria*

❾ Cervejaria Gazela

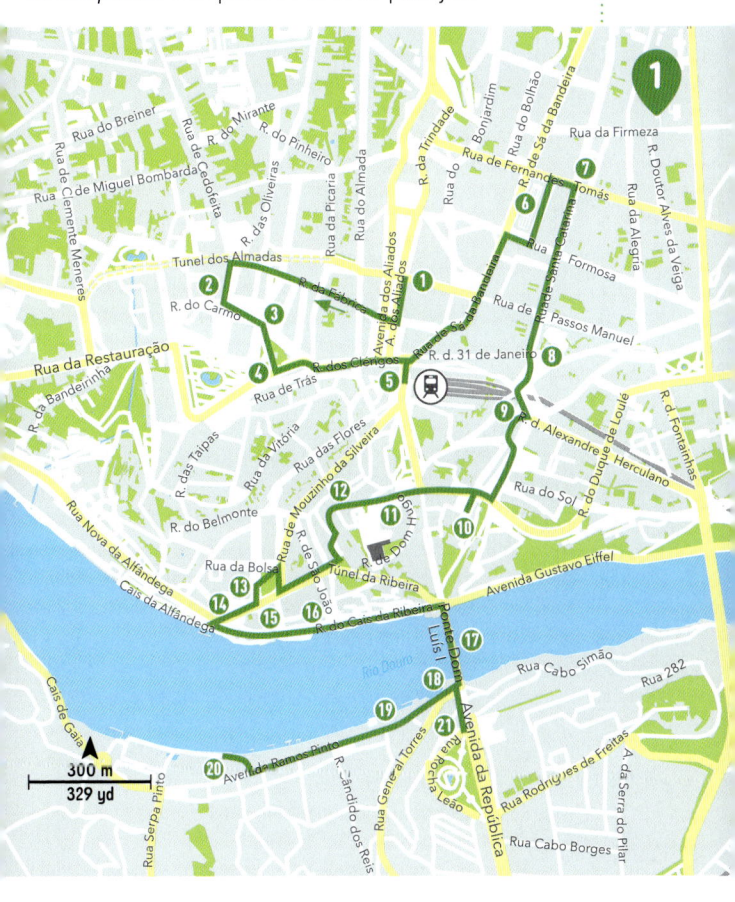

109

gazela.pt | €) has been serving delicious hotdogs, chips and *francesinhas* to generations of (mostly local) customers.

INSIDER TIP: Hotdogs for the hungry

FROM OLD TOWN TO RIVER
Pass the Teatro Nacional São João and Rua de Augusto Rosa to reach Largo 1° de Dezembro. While it might not look like anything special from the outside, a Baroque treasure awaits inside: the ⑩ **Igreja de Santa Clara ➤ p. 37** is brimming with *talha dourada*, the gold leaf sparkling once again after a long period of renovations. The cathedral ⑪ **Sé do Porto ➤ p. 38**, *which you can reach via Rua de Saraiva de Carvalho,* also received its fair share of gold during the Baroque period and has been repeatedly updated over the centuries.

- ⑩ Igreja de Santa Clara
- ⑪ Sé do Porto

INTO THE LABYRINTH
Head via Rua de Pena Ventosa and walk down into the ⑫ **Bairro da Sé ➤ p. 37**; once run-down and shabby, today it is charmingly picturesque. Keep an eye out for the *oratórios* – small, wooden house altars, some of which have been incorporated into granite niches. *Walk down Rua dos Mercadores and turn right at Túnel da Ribeira and you will soon find yourself at Praça do Infante Dom Henrique.* The prince, known in English as Henry the Navigator, looks resolutely towards the Atlantic, globe tucked under his arm. On the left stands the ostentatious ⑬ **Palácio da Bolsa ➤ p. 42**. The ⑭ **Igreja de São Francisco ➤ p. 42**, also Gothic on the outside and Baroque on the inside, is directly below and also dripping in gold leaf – they certainly didn't skimp on the decor here! *Around the corner once more you will find yourself standing by the river.* This is where the tour through the ⑮ **Ribeira district ➤ p. 40** gets under way, *from the medieval Rua da Reboleira to Praça da Ribeira.*

INSIDER TIP: Saints at home

- ⑫ Bairro da Sé
- ⑬ Palácio da Bolsa
- ⑭ Igreja de São Francisco
- ⑮ Ribeira district

SHIP AHOY!
Boats leave from the shore here; clamber on board for the hour-long ⑯ 🚩 **Cruzeiro das 6 Pontes** round trip. The tour will take you past all six bridges over the Douro

- ⑯ Cruzeiro das 6 Pontes

DISCOVERY TOURS

as well as numerous sights along the banks of Porto and Vila Nova de Gaia. You will even get a glimpse of the Atlantic. Explantory information is given in three languages (incl. English). Back on dry land, it is now time to cross the wrought-iron ⑰ **Ponte Dom Luís I** ➤ p. 39, which, incidentally, you will have just sailed under!

⑰ Ponte Dom Luís I

THE GRAND FINALE: THE BEST VIEW OF PORTO

A quick stroll along the ⑱ **Cais de Gaia** ➤ p. 54 in Vila Nova de Gaia will leave you with no doubt as to what this place is all about: port, port, port, as far as the eye can see. Make sure you try it for yourself in one of the ⑲ **port cellars** ➤ p. 53 on the waterfront. If your legs are getting tired, *take the* ⑳ *Teleférico de Gaia* ➤ p. 52 *and glide your way up to the Jardim do Morro.* From here, the view is dominated by the mighty ㉑ **Mosteiro da Serra do Pilar** ➤ p. 52. From the monastery forecourt you get simply the best view of Porto, especially at sunset!

⑱ Cais de Gaia

⑲ port cellars
⑳ Teleférico de Gaia

㉑ Mosteiro da Serra do Pilar

❷ MATOSINHOS BY BIKE

➤ **Indulge in beaches galore and fresh fish in Matosinhos**
➤ **Cycle the magnificent coastal bike path from Leça da Palmeira**
➤ **Discover Portugal's largest urban park**

📍	Dourobike bicycle rental	🏁	Dourobike bicycle rental
⟳	approx. 20 km	🚲	1 day (total cycling time approx. 2 hrs)

ℹ Try to reserve your bike a few days in advance from *Dourobike (Mon–Fri 10.30am–1.30pm and 2.30–6.30pm, Sat by appointment | Rua do Coronel Raúl Peres 100 | Foz do Douro | tel. 9 66 32 54 43 | dourobike.com).* And don't forget your swimsuit, especially in summer!

VAMOS À PRAIA!

Start your day at ❶ **Dourobike** in the chic suburb of Foz do Douro. Bike rented, *cycle north along the Atlantic*

❶ Dourobike

② **Forte de São Francisco Xavier**

③ **Praia de Matosinhos**

④ **Monumento Tragédia no Mar**

⑤ **Terminal de Cruzeiros**

⑥ **Jardim do Senhor do Padrão**

⑦ **Mercado de Matosinhos**

⑧ **Ponte Móvel**

coast. You'll pass various strips of beach until you reach ② **Forte de São Francisco Xavier ➤ p. 51**, otherwise known as the "Cheese Castle". *Not long after and you will have left Porto altogether!* The next beach, the vast ③ **Praia de Matosinhos**, is part of the neighbouring town of Matosinhos. A broad seafront promenade runs parallel to the beach and is rarely overcrowded, even in summer! At its end, next to the tourist information office, you'll find the ④ **Monumento Tragédia no Mar**, which commemorates the tragic events of December 1947 when 152 fishermen lost their lives in a storm. From here you have a cracking view of the futuristic ⑤ **Terminal de Cruzeiros**, architect Luís Pedro Silva's cruise terminal, like a giant white ribbon wrapped around the pier, which was inaugurated in 2015.

Cycle through the small ⑥ **Jardim do Senhor do Padrão** *and you will reach the restaurant district, conveniently located right next to the fishing port.* As you might imagine, one fish restaurant follows the next; the aroma of grilled sardines hanging in the air. And speaking of food, *turn the corner onto Avenida Engenheiro Duarte Pacheco* and you'll come to the ⑦ **Mercado de Matosinhos ➤ p. 83**. Over two levels you will discover whatever your heart desires: from live chickens and fresh fish to plant seeds and gourmet jams. Nowadays, you can pause for a quick bite to eat or even visit an art gallery!

INSIDER TIP
Art at the market

BACK TO THE BEACH VIA THE RIO LEÇA

From time to time, a container ship will pass through the ⑧ **Ponte Móvel**, a hydraulic bridge built in 2007 just behind the market building, and you will have to wait for it to reopen or, rather, close! From here, you can

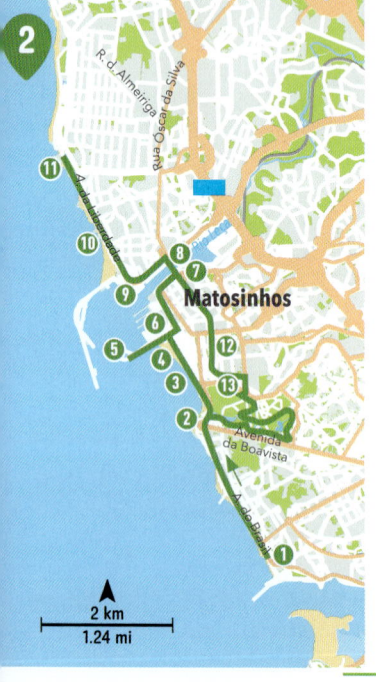

DISCOVERY TOURS

A stone memorial to the tragic events of 1947

watch the comings and goings of Portugal's largest container port, ❾ Porto de Leixões. *Continue along the shore* to see the vast breakwater moles, the old harbour fortress of Leça da Palmeira and the closest beaches. The seafront promenade *leading north takes you past the recently renovated tidal pool* ❿ Piscina das Marés *(open daily in bathing season 9am–7pm | 8 euros, Sat/Sun 10 euros)*, which dates back to the 1960s and was designed by architect Álvaro Siza Vieira.

Just next to the lighthouse of Leça is the very special and luxurious ⓫ Casa de Chá da Boa Nova *(closed Sun/Mon | Avenida da Liberdade 1681 | tel. 2 29 94 00 66 | casadechadaboanova.pt | €€€)*. The "House of Tea", also the work of star architect Siza Vieira, is built directly on the rocks, just two metres above the water. Today, Michelin-starred chef Rui Paula channels his artistry into the sophisticated restaurant, which has made a nationwide name for itself as an excellent seafood restaurant. Take a few pictures on the rocks and then head *back along the promenade* to Matosinhos.

❾ Porto de Leixões

❿ Piscina das Marés

⓫ Casa de Chá da Boa Nova

ARCHITECTURE AND NATURE

Cross the Ponte Móvel and cycle straight on along Rua Álvaro Castelões, which turns into Rua Mouzinho de Albuquerque. Turn right at Avenida Menéres and stop to visit the ⑫ Casa da Arquitectura *(Tue–Fri 10am–5pm, 10am–7pm in summer, Sat/Sun 10am–6pm, until 8pm in summer | 8 euros | Avenida Menéres 456 | casadaarquitectura.pt).* This modern architecture museum hosts both permanent and temporary exhibitions (including, of course, on Álvaro Siza Vieria) and is housed in an old wine warehouse of Real Companhia Vinícola. *Cycle down Rua Dom João I, the Passeio da Praia cycle path and a short stretch of Estrada da Circunvalação and you will reach the green lung of Porto:* ⑬ Parque da Cidade ➤ p. 51. *Complete a lap of the park before returning to the riverside promenade cycling back to* ❶ Dourobike.

③ PORTO'S LESSER-KNOWN EAST SIDE

➤ Go for a stroll away from the tourist hotspots
➤ Stumble upon unexpected views over the Douro
➤ Climb a hill on quaint stairways

📍 Jardim de São Lázaro
→ approx. 4 km

🏁 Estação de Campanhã
🚶 ½ day (total walking time approx 1¼ hrs)

UNEXPECTED VIEWS

If you want to escape the tourist hotspots of the city centre, go east! Join the locals in the cosy ❶ Jardim de São Lázaro, which was inaugurated in 1834 as Porto's first public park. This end of town, you might spot the pupils from the Colégio Nossa Senhora da Esperança, whose Baroque façade bears the signature of the great master Nicolau Nasoni. *Pass the Catholic school on your right and continue south along Rua das Fontaínhas until you reach* ❷ Miradouro das Fontaínhas. Here you will be treated to spectacular views of the river and

DISCOVERY TOURS

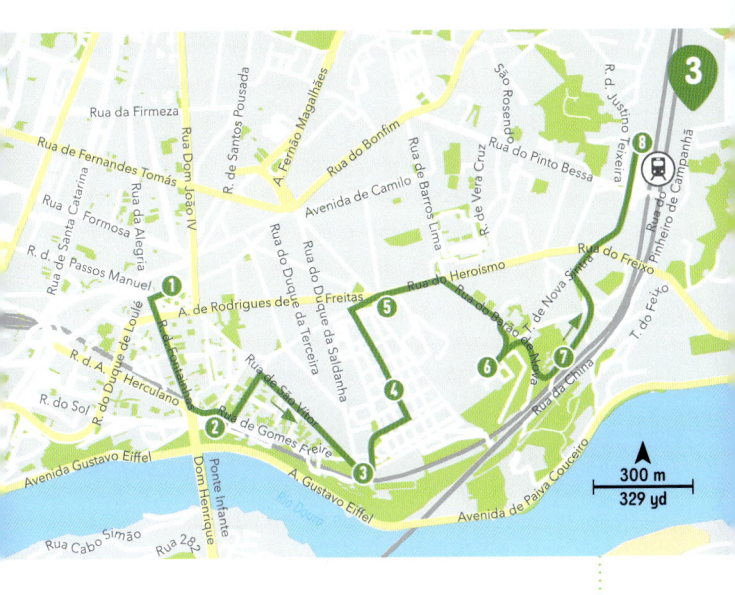

the Ponte Dona Maria Pia, built by Gustave Eiffel in 1877. It was once the largest arch bridge in the world, but by 1991 it was no longer suitable for modern trains and was closed. Now, just like the former Ramal da Alfândega railway line running below the lookout point, it is awaiting its resurrection as a pedestrian and cycle route.

THE OLDEST CEMETARY IN PORTO

Take the Praça da Alegria and then Rua de São Vítor. On this street there are more than 20 *ilhas* (19th-century working-class housing complexes). If you're lucky, someone might leave a door open and you can have a look inside. At the end of the street is the school of the Salesian order. Next to what is surely the city's most picturesque school sports field, you too can enjoy the view from the ❸ Miradouro dos Salesianos. Next, *take the south entrance* into the ❹ Cemitério do Prado do Repouso, which was inaugurated in 1839. Wander among the elaborate tombs and centuries-old trees in this old municipal cemetery. *Leave through the north entrance.*

❸ Miradouro dos Salesianos

❹ Cemitério do Prado do Repouso

115

⑤ Museu Militar do Porto

On your right, you'll see the ⑤ **Museu Militar do Porto** *(Tue–Sun 10am–12.30pm and 2–5pm | 3 euros | Rua do Heroísmo 329)*. During the dictatorship of Salazar, the building was used by the PIDE, the secret police. Once you have visited, *walk the short distance along Rua do Heroísmo and then turn right into Rua do Barão de Nova Sintra.* Behind the waterworks, which includes the lovely ⑥ **Parque das Águas** *(April–Sept daily 9am–7pm, Oct–March 10am–6pm | free admission),* you will enter a different world: stairs line the ⑦ **Travessa da China** alleyway which leads *down on the left* to an old, almost village-like working-class district on the hillside. China here doesn't refer to the country, but to the porcelain that was once made here. The place is a world apart, and yet it's just a five-minute walk from Porto's main train station ⑧ **Estação de Campanhã**, which, incidentally, you will reach shortly afterwards.

⑥ Parque das Águas

⑦ Travessa da China

⑧ Estação de Campanhã

④ PORTO'S STREET ART

➤ **Explore Porto's colourful walls and creative installations**
➤ **Follow in the footsteps of the city's most famous street artists**
➤ **See how rubbish becomes art in Vila Nova de Gaia**

📍 Trindade car park   🏁 Cais de Gaia

➡ A good 5km   🚶 ½ day (total walking time approx. 1½ hrs)

❶ Trindade multi-storey car park

On the side of the ❶ **Trindade multistorey car park**, is the city's first officially commissioned graffiti wall: back in 2014, Porto street artist MrDheo *(@mrdheo)* immortalised his father, who is depicted holding a spray can in one hand and the Torre dos Clérigos in the other. More recent is the graffiti work on the south side. This is the 2021 creation of Lisbon artist Tamara Alves *(tamaraalves.com)* and is a commentary on European social rights. *Head down Rua do Doutor Ricardo Jorge until you reach Rua da Conceição,* where it's worth glancing into the ❷ **shopping arcade** at number 80: Polish artist Dasior *(@dasior_tattoo)* and Porto native Nuno

❷ shopping arcade

DISCOVERY TOURS

Look out for this cat on a side alley off Rua das Flores

Costah *(costah.net)* joined forces in 2017 to create this rather attractive fish landscape. *Carry on along Rua de José Falcão to Rua Actor João Guedes,* where your eye will be drawn to the bright ❸ **tiled wall** on the side of a steakhouse by famous artist Joana Vasconcelos. *Follow Rua da Fábrica back to Avenida dos Aliados and the north side of São Bento station:* 3,000 azulejos over a space of 135 m² at 182 Rua da Madeira seek to answer the question ❹ **Quem és, Porto?** (Who are you, Porto?), posed by urban artist ±maismenos± *(maismenos.net).*

❸ tiled wall

❹ Quem és, Porto?

LOOK ME IN THE EYE, KITTY!
At the front of the station, turn into Rua das Flores. The street, in places adorned with kitsch plastic flowers, is a work of art in itself. The most eye-catching work is the giant ❺ **blue cat** the size of a house by Galician artist Liqen *(@liqen).* The cat's yellow eyes follow you from *the narrow side street Rua Afonso Martins Alho. Keep right at the end of Rua das Flores. Just a few metres further and it's right again up the Escadas da Vitória.* Your

❺ blue cat

117

- ⑥ Miradouro da Vitória
- ⑦ Faceless Madonna
- ⑧ Rua da Ancira 6-8
- ⑨ Mira

first reward is the view at the ⑥ **Miradouro da Vitória** and then from the **Passeio das Virtudes**. Here the painting of the ⑦ **Faceless Madonna** by enterprising Porto artist Hazul *(hazul.pt)* is on display at the Árvore art school.

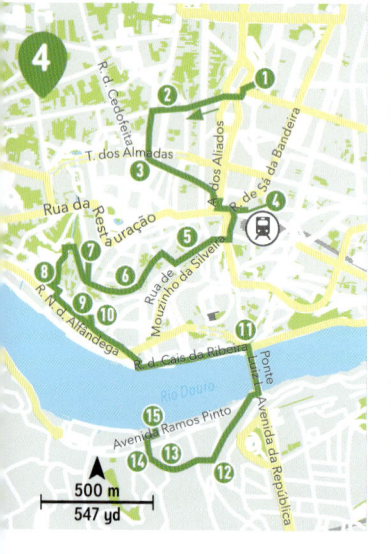

Head along Calçada das Virtudes then down to Miragaia, where Lisbon artist Vhils designed the striking façade at ⑧ **Rua da Ancira 6-8** using his well-known scratch-the-surface technique, where he creates enormous portraits by chiselling away bits of plaster. *Walk along Rua de Miragaia and you will reach Largo de Artur Arcos* and the graffito ⑨ **Mira** by Daniel Eime. This portrait of an older woman is the artist's homage to the older generation. *Just around the corner,* take a seat on the terrace of music café ⑩ **Mirajazz** *(Tue–Sun 3–9pm | Escadas do Caminho Novo 11 | FB)* and listen to afternoon jazz with the most delightful view of the river. Next, *stroll east along Cais da*

DISCOVERY TOURS

Stroll along the Cais da Ribeira towards the Ponte Dom Luís I

Ribeira to see the 40m-long tile piece called ⑪ **Ribeira Negra**, which was designed by renowned Portuguese artist Júlio Resende (1917–2011) in 1984 and is right next to the Ribeira tunnel.

COLOURFUL CORNERS IN VILA NOVA DE GAIA
Now *cross the Dom Luís I bridge onto Rua do General Torres, and head down the* ⑫ **Escadaria da Travessa de Cândido dos Reis** where bright miniature façades adorn the stair landings; even the associated painters are immortalised here. *Head along Rua de Guilherme Braga until you reach the parish church of Santa Marinha. Behind the church* is a beautifully painted little ⑬ **transformer house** with delicate floral motifs – the work of Argentinean artist Pastel. *Next take Rua Dom Afonso III towards the river* and you will see the giant ⑭ **Half Rabbit** on the first corner. The rabbit is the creation of Lisbon street artist and environmental activist Bordalo II and is made from rubbish and paint. *Just a few metres further and you will find yourself on the riverside promenade* ⑮ **Cais de Gaia.**

⑩ Mirajazz
⑪ Ribeira Negra

⑫ Escada da Travessa de Cândido dos Reis

⑬ transformer house

⑭ Half Rabbit

⑮ Cais de Gaia

119

GOOD TO KNOW
CITY BREAK BASICS

ARRIVAL

GETTING THERE

Assuming you haven't embarked on a lengthy road trip or cruise, you will probably get to Porto by plane. In theory, you can travel by train or bus from the UK, but these alternatives are both time-consuming and usually more expensive.

TAP Portugal as well as low-cost airlines like Ryanair and Easyjet all fly in and out of *Porto's Aeroporto Francisco Sá Carneiro (ana.pt)*, which is located some 12km north of the city centre.

> **Time zone**
>
> Portugal runs on Greenwich Mean Time, so British and Irish visitors don't need to reset their watches.

The best way to reach the centre from the airport is by metro (6am to 12.40am); choose price zone Z 4 (currently 2.25 euros). City buses 601 and 602 also run between the city centre (terminus: Cordoaria) and the airport from 5.30am to midnight for the same price. At other times (i.e. between 12.30am and 5.30am), opt for the hourly 3M bus to Avenida dos Aliados. By bus, the trip usually takes somewhere between half an hour and 45 minutes.

A taxi is likely to take just as long in the evening rush hour, but outside peak times some drivers can make it in under half an hour. Depending on the time of day, a taxi to the city centre will set you back between 20 and 35 euros; ride-hailing apps such as Uber are usually a bit cheaper.

Excursion boats are a popular way to see the river and the city

ENTRY REQUIREMENTS

EU citizens and Swiss nationals can use an identity card or passport to enter Portugal. Visitors from non-EU countries need a passport to enter. US and UK citizens can travel visa-free to Portugal for stays of up to 90 days.

CLIMATE & WHEN TO GO

Admittedly, you can't guarantee good weather in March, but you do know it won't be very busy yet and the camellia trees will be in full bloom. It gets very crowded between May and September, the classic months for city trips. From May to July Porto also hosts several music festivals and, in particular, the São João celebrations on 24 June. In short, it gets busy! If swimming is on your agenda, aim for August or September, by which point the Atlantic will have warmed up to a still-refreshing 18°C and the air temperature will have reached 25–30°C. A trip to the surrounding wine regions is worthwhile in late summer when the grapes are harvested. While the city is definitely less crowded in winter, you might want to avoid the fog-enshrouded Atlantic city between November and February. Of course, you will still get plenty of clear and sunny days in winter, but you might be doomed to a week of rain. On New Year's Eve, there is a huge party on Avenida dos Aliados with the most spectacular fireworks. Still, overall Porto is definitely more beautiful in the sunshine.

INSIDER TIP *Camellias in the spring*

GETTING AROUND

CAR

Car traffic is heavily restricted in some parts of the city centre (Ribeira, Santa Catarina, Cedofeita and around Rua das Flores) and it's best to avoid driving into the centre altogether. The speed limit in built-up areas is 50kmh, on rural roads it's 90kmh or, where indicated, 100kmh, and on motorways it's a maximum of 120kmh. Remember that *auto-estradas* (motorways) are subject to tolls; some have no toll booths and you need to register electronically. If you do use one of these routes – or if you use the "Via Verde" lane on conventional toll booth routes – you will need a small electronic toll-reader box. You can rent one from car hire companies for around 2 euros per day.

CAR HIRE

Hiring a car is a good option if you are hoping to explore the area around Porto (e.g. the Douro Valley) as well as the city itself. But if you're going to stay central, a car will only be a hindrance; parking spaces are rare and expensive and streets are often congested. If you're in the Old Town district, you don't stand a chance – and that's putting it politely! If you're still determined to rent a car, your best bet is to reserve one in advance. Pick your car up either at the airport or at one of the hire company's branches in the city. Prices vary hugely between high and low season. If you plan to use the motorways, the car will need an electronic toll reader (see above).

Heritage trams still trundle through the city as part of the transport network

GOOD TO KNOW

PUBLIC TRANSPORT
You can reach almost every corner of the city as well as the surrounding areas by bus, tram or metro. The dense network of city buses and the three historic tram lines 1, 18 and 22 are operated by STCP *(stcp.pt)*. A single fare on the tram is 5 euros and 2.50 euros on the bus. STCP also operates the Funicular dos Guindais for 4 euros a ticket. Outside the city centre, the metro *(metrodoporto.pt)*, which was inaugurated in 2002, is mostly above ground. The six lines (A–F) run between 6am and 1am. To use the metro, you need a *Cartão Andante (linhandante.com, metrodoporto.pt/pages/287)* ticket. The card itself costs 60 cents and can then be loaded for one year with single, multiple or 24-hour tickets at the ticket vending machines inside the metro stations or at Loja Andante outlets. For unlimited use of the metro, buses, and some regional trains to get around the city, the

> **INSIDER TIP: Andante Tour card**
> *Andante Tour 1* is a great option: it costs just 7 euros and is valid for 24 hours from validation.

Andante Tour 3 costs 15 euros and lasts 72 hours. Both tickets are valid for travel up to zone Z 4 (i.e. to the airport), but not for the tram or funicular. Neither card can be recharged. The soon-to-be inaugurated hydrogen-powered metroBus should reduce traffic on Avenida Boavista.

TAXIS
Taxis in Portugal are cheaper than in the UK, averaging around 50 cents per kilometre. You will have to pay a surcharge for ordering by phone (e.g. on *tel. 2 25 07 64 00*), or for late-night trips or pieces of luggage. Taxi ranks, or *praças de taxi*, can be found at e.g. São Bento station or on Rua do Infante Dom Henrique near the Ribeira, or can be hailed down in the street. As a rule, taxis are metred. Ride-hailing services such as Uber are usually even cheaper, and you can order and pay for your taxi on the corresponding apps.

EMERGENCIES

EMBASSIES & CONSULATES
UK EMBASSY
Rua de São Bernardo 33, 1249-082 Lisbon | tel. 2 13 92 40 00 | gov.uk/world/organisations/british-embassy-lisbon

US EMBASSY
Avenida das Forças Armadas | 1600-081 Lisboa | tel. 2 17 27 33 00 | pt.usembassy.gov

EMERGENCY NUMBERS
Dial *112* for police, fire brigade and ambulance.

HEALTH
UK travellers can use a UK Global Health Insurance Card (GHIC) to obtain basic emergency healthcare at A&E *(urgência)* or the public hospital *(hospital)*. In the centre of Porto, this is the Hospital de Santo António; in the north of the city, it is the Hospital de

São João. However, you are also advised to take out private travel insurance before travelling. EU residents can use the European Health Insurance Card (EHIC); the costs are refunded in keeping with the rates in your home country. Travel insurance is necessary for any additional services. Be sure to keep the doctor's report and the bill to submit to your health insurance company. Pharmacies are called *farmácias*. You do need a prescription for antibiotics, but many other medications are available without one.

ESSENTIALS

ACCOMMODATION

Porto is sure to have what you're looking for, from simple hotels or youth hostels *(pousadasjuventude.pt)* to chic boutique or luxury hotels. Renting private apartments through platforms like Airbnb is popular in the city centre, and it is becoming more and more common for local living space, sometimes entire neighbourhoods, to be taken over by holiday accommodation. If you want to avoid fuelling this, a hotel or hostel is usually the fairer option. There are even campsites outside the city, especially near the beaches of Vila Nova de Gaia.

BEACHES

The Atlantic can be treacherous, so make sure you follow the lifeguards' instructions and flags: green = all good, yellow = caution, red = no bathing. Remember, however, that the lifeguards only operate in summer. Also note the tidal range: the difference between high and low tide can be almost 3m depending on the phase of the moon. You can consult a tide table, for example at *hidrografico.pt*. You can also check out the waves and surfing conditions at Matosinhos beach with the webcam *beachcam.meo.pt*. While there are no official nudist beaches in the greater Porto area, nude bathing is tolerated at the very natural Praia do Cabedelo, on the south bank of the Douro estuary.

CUSTOMS

Goods for personal use may be imported and exported duty-free within the EU. Guidelines are, for example, 800 cigarettes, 10 litres of spirits and up to 20 litres of port. UK citizens can import and export for their personal use tax-free: 200 cigarettes or 250g tobacco, 4 litres of spirits or 9 litres of fortified wine over 22%. For further information, go to *gov.uk/bringing-goods-into-uk-personal-use*

RESPONSIBLE TRAVEL

Don't just think about your carbon footprint when flying to and from your holiday destination, but also about how you can protect nature and culture abroad. As a tourist it is especially important to respect nature, look out for local products, cycle instead of drive, save water and much more. To find out more about eco-tourism please visit: *ecotourism.org*

GOOD TO KNOW

INFORMATION
The official website of the municipal tourism office (including a chat feature) is *visitporto.travel*. There are local tourist information offices in several places, e.g. at the airport *(daily 9am-6pm)* and next to the cathedral *(daily 9am-6pm | Torre Medieval | ɰ j7)*. The interactive *Porto Welcome Center (daily 9am-7pm | Praçeta Almeida Garrett 27 | ɰ j6)* is opposite São Bento station.

PUBLIC HOLIDAYS

1 Jan	New Year's Day
March/April	Good Friday
25 April	Anniversary of the 1974 Carnation Revolution
1 May	Labour Day
May/June	Corpus Christi
10 June	Portugal Day
24 June	São João (feast day of the city's patron saint)
15 Aug	Assumption
5 Oct	Portugal Republic Day
1 Nov	All Saints' Day
1 Dec	Restoration of Independence Day
8 Dec	Feast of the Immaculate Conception
25 Dec	Christmas

LUGGAGE STORAGE
If you have to check out of your (private) accommodation in the morning, but your flight home isn't until the evening, you can store your luggage at one of the six *Citylockers (citylockers.pt)* locations. You can also find luggage storage nearby using *luggagehero.com* or *usebounce.com*; these are often located in small cafés or shops. *Luggit (luggit.app)* will come to you to pick up your luggage and return it wherever you want. They also accept large items such as surfboards.

MONEY & CREDIT CARDS
Portugal's national currency is the euro. You can find *Multibanco* ATMs all over the city. Bank fees may apply (check with your bank) and there may be a daily withdrawal limit. You can pay for almost everything by credit or debit card, incl. rental cars, hotels and often restaurants.

HOW MUCH DOES IT COST?

Coffee	*from 0.70 euros for an espresso*
Wine	*from 5 euros for 1 litre of house wine in a simple restaurant*
Azulejos	*from 5 euros for a painted tile*
Food	*from 8 euros for a daily special*
Bus	*2.50 euros for a single fare on a city bus*
Bicycle	*around 15 euros for a day's rental*

OPENING HOURS
Most shops open for business Monday to Saturday from 10am to 7/8pm, sometimes with a lunch break (1-2pm). The big shopping centres open seven days a week from 10am to 11pm. Supermarkets often stay open on Sundays and until 9pm in the evenings. Some museums close on Mondays, and many of the smaller

ones close for lunch. Opening hours vary depending on the season; in summer, attractions usually stay open later. Some restaurants also vary their opening hours between high and low season, and many local, family-run restaurants close on Sundays.

PORTO CARD

If you plan to visit several museums or attractions in Porto, it is probably worth your while picking up a *Porto Card (short.travel/prt2)*. The card offers a range of discounts at monuments, museums, port cellars, shops, restaurants, event venues and on boat tours. It costs 25 euros for three days and includes all means of public transport except the tram, making it only 10 euros more than the *Andante Tour 3* public transport card (see p. 123). There are also one-day, two-day and four-day options, as well as options that do not include public transport.

POST

Post offices (and boxes) are a familiar red and are called *CTT* or *correios*. Most open Monday to Friday from 9am to 6pm. You can also buy stamps from vending machines and in some souvenir shops. Find a branch and postal rates at *ctt.pt*.

PRICES

Prices can vary dramatically even within individual hotels; a room in high season may well cost twice as much as in winter. While public transport is cheaper than in the UK, some foods and especially cosmetics (think sun cream!) are more expensive in

WEATHER IN PORTO

■ High season
■ Low season

	JAN	FEB	MARCH	APRIL	MAY	JUNE	JULY	AUG	SEPT	OCT	NOV	DEC
Daytime temperature	14°	15°	17°	18°	20°	23°	25°	25°	23°	21°	17°	15°
Night-time temperature	6°	7°	8°	9°	12°	14°	15°	15°	14°	12°	9°	7°
Hours of sunshine per day	4	5	5	5	7	8	10	9	8	5	5	4
Rainy days per month	15	13	13	15	14	8	7	7	10	16	16	17
Water temperature in °C	14°	14°	14°	15°	17°	17°	17°	18°	18°	18°	17°	16°

GOOD TO KNOW

Portugal. The fairly ubiquitous German discounters are cheaper than normal supermarkets. Luckily, museums are affordable; as a rule, a ticket (which often includes a guided tour) costs between 3 and 10 euros, with discounts available for children, students and senior citizens. The various branches of the city museum charge 4 euros each, while the combined ticket for the entire Museu do Porto costs 8 euros, and some sections are even free of charge. Family attractions are, however, expensive.

SAFETY
Portugal is a relatively safe holiday destination and has mercifully been spared from terrorist attacks so far. The best way to protect yourself from pickpockets is to wear your backpack on your front in crowds and avoid carrying any valuables with you. Take particular care on crowded buses, trams and the metro, as well as at markets and major festivals. If something does happen, contact the *PSP (Policia de Segurança Pública)*, the *Esquadra de Turismo* is located on *Praça de Pedro Nunes 16 (buses Igreja Cedofeita | tel. 2 22 09 20 06 | G4)*.

TELEPHONE & INTERNET
The dialling code for Portugal is 00351; there are no dialling codes within Portugal. Portuguese mobile phone numbers begin with 9; landline numbers with 2. If you don't want to use up all your mobile data, there should be Wi-Fi in every hotel as well as in most restaurants and cafés.

TIPPING
Five to ten per cent is the norm in a restaurant, provided you were satisfied with the service. Just leave coins on the table at the end. Cleaning staff and porters in hotels are also happy to receive a small tip.

TOILETS
In many older toilets and in some beach bars, the thin pipes can't cope with loo paper. If that's the case, it should go in the bin by the toilet.

WATER
The tap water is perfectly safe to drink but you can sometimes taste a hint of chlorine. Bottled water is available from the supermarket.

Café Majestic

WORDS & PHRASES IN PORTUGUESE

SMALL TALK

yes/no/maybe	sim/não/talvez
please	se faz favor
thank you	obrigado (m)/obrigada (f)
Good morning!/day!/evening!/night!	Bom dia!/Bom dia!/Boa tarde!/Boa noite!
Hello!/Hi!	Olá!/Cião!
My name is …	Chamo-me …
What's your name?	Como te chamas?/Como se chama?
I'm from…	Sou de …
Excuse me!	Desculpa!/Desculpe!
Pardon?	Como?
I (don't) like that	(Não) Gosto disto
good/bad	bem/mal

SYMBOLS

EATING & DRINKING

The menu, please	A ementa, se faz favor
bottle/glass	garrafa/copo
salt/pepper/sugar	sal/pimenta/açúcar
vinegar/oil	vinagre/azeite
knife/fork/spoon	faca/garfo/colher
milk/cream/lemom	leite/nata/limão
with/without ice/gas	com/sem gelo/gás
vegetarian/allergic	vegetariano/a alérgico/a
bill	conta
I would like to pay, please	A conta, se faz favor
with cash/with credit card	em dinheiro/com cartão de crédito

MISCELLANEOUS

Where is …?/Where are …?	Onde é …?/Onde são …?
What time is it?	Que horas são?
It's 3 o'clock	São três horas
today/tomorrow/yesterday	hoje/amanhã/ontem
How much is …?	Quanto custa …?
Where can I find internet access?	Onde há acesso à internet?
Help!/Attention!	Socorro!/Atenção!
fever/pain	febre/dores
pharmacy/chemist	farmácia/drogaria
ban/forbidden	interdição/proibido
broken/not working	estragado/não funciona
breakdown/workshop	avaria/garagem
timetable/ticket	horário/bilhete
0/1/2/3/4/5/6/7/8/9/ 10/100/1000	zero/um, uma/dois, duas/três/quatro/cinco/seis/sete/oito/nove/dez/ cem/mil

HOLIDAY VIBES
FOR RELAXATION & CHILLING

FOR BOOKWORMS & FILM BUFFS

📖 THE MISSING HEAD OF DAMASCENO MONTEIRO
Italian writer Antonio Tabucchi's 1997 crime novel set in Porto is a chilling tribute to the city on the Douro and a country so close the author's heart. Tabloid journalist Firmino becomes a champion of justice when he finds himself investigating the case of a floating corpse.

🎥 PORTO
This romantic drama (2016) from Gabe Klinger tells the opposites-attract story of two strangers: Jake is the introverted son of an Anglo-Saxon diplomat, while French archaeologist Mati is brimming with self-confidence. After meeting in Porto and spending the night together, they find themselves unable to forget one another.

📖 HUNTING MIDNIGHT
Richard Zimler's 2004 epic novel is a love story in which the action takes place against a backdrop of slavery and religious oppression. It's partly set in Porto's riverine Ribeira district at the turn of the 19th century.

PLAYLIST ON SHUFFLE

0:58

▌ **PEDRO ABRUNHOSA** – PARA OS BRAÇOS DA MINHA MÃE
This pop and jazz musician has a beautiful velvety voice. He sings here of his yearning for his mother.

▶ **RUI VELOSO** – ANEL DE RUBÍ
This rock and blues singer is the father of Portuguese rock, and Porto plays a starring role in many of his songs.

▶ **GNR** – DUNAS
The band has been rocking the country since the early 1980s.

▶ **ORNATOS VIOLETA** – DEIXA MORRER
This alternative rock band from the 1990s is touring the festivals again and is more popular than ever.

▶ **BLIND ZERO** – SHINE ON
This grunge and rock band has been a fixture in Portugal's charts since 1994.

The holiday soundtrack is available on **Spotify** under **MARCO POLO Portugal**

Or scan this code with the Spotify app

ONLINE

TIMEOUT.PT/PORTO
Online version of the events magazine. Features all the latest recommendations for activities, event, cafés, restaurants, shops and accommodation.

AGENDACULTURALPORTO.ORG
Portuguese calendar of events, including online ticket links for lots of attractions.

EXPATNETWORK.COM/ LIFE-IN-PORTUGAL
Dives a little deeper into everyday life in Portugal.

SHORT.TRAVEL/POR1
A hefty YouTube introduction to the world of port.

PORTOALITIES.COM
Check out this useful blog written by a Porto local, offering tourist information, insider tips and specialist tour bookings.

IPMA.PT
What about the weather? Check the Portuguese national meteorological website here.

TRAVEL PURSUIT
THE MARCO POLO HOLIDAY QUIZ

Do you know what makes Porto tick? Here you can test your knowledge of the idiosyncrasies and eccentricities of the city and its people. The answers are at the bottom of the page, with further details on pages 20 to 25 of this guide.

❶ What gives Porto such a special atmosphere?
a) The remarkable number of Romanesque buildings
b) Its fantastic location on both the Douro river and the Atlantic
c) The many vineyards growing port grapes around the city

❷ Why were churches decorated with *azulejos*?
a) They're practical – easy to wipe clean
b) To tell biblical stories in place of frescoes
c) To brighten up the dark granite walls

❸ What is the Escola do Porto?
a) A centuries-old college for oenologists
b) The FC Porto academy founded by José Mourinho
c) A 20th-century movement in modern Portuguese architecture

❹ Why did so many English wine merchants settle in Porto in the 18th century?
a) Only the English had the wine-making knowledge for port back then
b) Because of the prohibition introduced in England at the time
c) Because the Methuen Treaty eliminated both customs duties and trade restrictions between Portugal and England

Answers: 1b, 2b, 3c, 4c, 5a, 6b, 7a, 8a, 9c, 10b

The vines for port production grow on the banks of the Douro, but where exactly?

❺ How did King Dom Pedro IV thank the city of Porto for its support during the Miguelist War?
a) He bequeathed the city his heart
b) With a handsome donation to build the Palácio da Bolsa
c) He awarded the city the title *Cidade Invicta* ("Invincible City")

❻ Where are the grapes for port grown?
a) To the south of the city, behind the port cellars of Vila Nova de Gaia
b) Some 100km upriver in the Alto Douro
c) In the vineyards of Porto, especially in the Parque da Cidade

❼ What is the original meaning of the word *azulejo* (from the Arabic *al-zulij*)?
a) Small, polished stone
b) Blue tile
c) Shiny tile

❽ What is Porto's long-distance runner Rosa Mota campaigning for?
a) For the Portuguese to get more exercise
b) For the Olympics to be held in Portugal
c) As a curator, for a good programme in the event space that bears her name

❾ What is *talha dourada*?
a) A compoent of *francesinha*
b) The golden-red glow of the Atlantic at sunset
c) The gold leaf-covered woodcarvings found in so many of Portugal's churches

❿ Which is the must-have accessory for the São João city festival in June?
a) Deep-fried, filled doughnuts
b) A plastic hammer
c) A neckerchief with the city's coat of arms

INDEX

Alfândega Nova 43, 101
Alfândega Régia 59
Arrábida 45
Ascensor da Ribeira 41
Avenida dos Aliado 121
Avenida dos Aliados 30, 101, 108, 120
Bairro da Sé 18, 37, 38, 110
Bairro do Barredo 41
Baixa 27, 30
Banco de Materiais 11, 36
Batalha Centro de Cinema 100
Boavista 45
Cais de Gaia 54, 111, 119
Câmara Municipal 30
Canidelo 98
Capela das Almas de Santa Catarina 109
Capela do Socorro 59
Capela Santa Catarina 55
Cartão Andante 123
Casa Andresen 47
Casa da Arquitectura 114
Casa da Música 10, 18, 47, 94, 101
Casa de Chá 56
Casa de Chá da Boa Nova 113
Casa do Cinema Manoel de Oliveira 56
Casa do Infante 11, 41
Casa Escondida 36
Casa Marta Ortigão Sampaio 48
Casa Serralves 56
Casa Tait 45
Castelo do Queijo 51
Cedofeita 30
Cemitério do Prado do Repouso 115
Centro Interpretativo do Património da Afurada 58
Centro Português de Fotografia 11, 33
Cine-Teatro Batalha 32
Convento de Corpus Christi 54, 101
Cruzeiro das 6 Pontes 13, 110
Douro (see Rio Douro)
Douro Promenade (Foz do Douro) 49
Elevador da Lada 41
Elizondo 108
Escadaria da Travessa de Cândido dos Reis 119
Estação de Campanhã 116
Estação de São Bento 13, 33, 108
Estádio do Bessa 98
Estádio do Dragão 21, 24, 56, 98
Estuário do Douro 58
Farol de São Miguel-o-Anjo 49
Farolim de Felgueiras 50
Fonte do Cubo 41

Forte de São Francisco Xavier 51, 112
Forte de São João Baptista 50
Foz do Douro 27, 48, 73, 90
Foz Velha 49
Funicular dos Guindais 38, 123
Galeria da Biodiversidade 11, 47
Igreja das Carmelitas 35
Igreja de Massarelos 46
Igreja de Santa Clara 25, 37, 110
Igreja de Santo Ildefonso 32, 109
Igreja de São Francisco 25, 42, 110
Igreja do Carmo 25, 35, 108
Igreja dos Clérigos 25, 34
Jardim Botânico do Porto 11, 46
Jardim das Sobreiras 49
Jardim de São Lázaro 114
Jardim do Calém 49
Jardim do Morro 52, 101
Jardim do Passeio Alegre 50
Jardim do Senhor do Padrão 112
Jardins do Palácio de Cristal 45, 101
Largo da Pena Ventosa 38
Leixões 113
Livraria Lello 10, 18, 34, 78, 108
Look at Porto 12, 55
Marégrafo 50
Matosinhos 66, 72, 100
Mercado de Matosinhos 112
Mercado do Bolhão 31, 82, 108
Miradouro das Fontaínhas 114
Miradouro da Vitória 118
Miradouro dos Salesianos 115
Mira (Graffito) 118
Monumento Tragédia no Mar 112
Mosteiro da Serra do Pilar 52, 101, 111
Muralha Fernandina 39
Muro dos Bacalhoeiros 41
Museu das Marionetas 42
Museu de Arte Contemporânea 55
Museu de História Natural e da Cincia 35
Museu do Carro Eléctrico 12, 46
Museu do Porto 11, 41, 127
Museu dos Transportes e Comunicações 43
Museu do Vinho do Porto 11, 13, 41
Museu do Vitral 38
Museu Futebol Clube do Porto 56
Museu Militar do Porto 116
Museu Nacional da Imprensa 57
Museu Nacional do Soares dos Reis 10, 37
Museu Romântico 45
Nau Quinhentista 59

Nossa Senhora da Guia 59
Paço Episcopal 38
Palácio da Bolsa 10, 42, 100, 101, 110
Palácio de Cristal 45
Pao Episcopal 38
Parque da Cidade 12, 51, 99, 100, 114
Parque das Águas 116
Parque de Serralves 27, 55, 100, 101
Passeio das Virtude 118
Pavilhão da Água 12, 52
Pavilhão Rosa Mota 45
Pelourinho 38
Pérgola da Foz 50
Piscina das Marés 113
Planetário do Porto 46
Ponte da Arrábida 98
Ponte do Infante 99
Ponte Dom Luís I 39, 111
Ponte Móvel 112
Ponte Pênsil 40
port cellars 53, 111
Porto Card 11, 126
Porto de Leixões 113
Praça da Batalha 32
Praça da Liberdade 30, 31
Praça da Ribeira 41
Praia de Lavadores 58
Praia de Matosinhos 99, 112
Praia do Cabedelo 50
Praia do Homem do Leme 12, 50
Praia do Senhor da Pedra 59
Quinta do Fojo 98
Ribeira 17, 18, 40, 110, 130
Rio Douro 16, 18, 20, 23, 26, 100
Rua das Flores 33
Santa Catarina 55
Santa Clara 37, 110
Santo Ildefonso 32, 109
São Bento 33, 108
São Pedro da Afurada 57, 58, 66, 99
Seafront Promenade 50
Sea Life 10, 51
Sé do Porto 25, 38, 110
Serralves 55
Tasca da Badalhoca 13, 71
Teatro Nacional São João 32
Teleférico de Gaia 52, 111
Terminal de Cruzeiros 112
Terreiro da Sé 38
Torre dos Clérigos 13, 34, 108
Travessa da China 116
Universidade do Porto 23, 35, 101
Vila do Conde 59
Vila Nova de Gaia 20, 23, 26, 52, 98, 101, 103
World of Discoveries 12, 43
World of Wine 55, 101

INDEX & CREDITS

WE WANT TO HEAR FROM YOU!

Did you have a great holiday? Is there something on your mind? Whatever it is, let us know! Whether you want to praise the guide, alert us to errors or give us a personal tip – MARCO POLO would be pleased to hear from you.

Please contact us by email:

sales@heartwoodpublishing.co.uk

We do everything we can to provide the very latest information for your trip. Nevertheless, despite all of our authors' thorough research, errors can creep in. MARCO POLO does not accept any liability for this.

PICTURE CREDITS
Cover photo: Church of Santo Ildefonso (AWL Images/ClickAlps)
Photos: L. Forst-Gill/F. Beuerskens (2/3, 13, 31, 36, 65, 66, 79, 90/91, 104/105, 130/131); Huber-images: L. Debelkova (outside front flap/1), Eiben (16/17, 26/27), M. Howard (34/35), S. Lubenow (60/61), R. Schmid (4, 8/9, 12, 40, 43, 74/75), J. Wlodarczyk (22); Laif: J. Schwarz (94), G. Standl (71, 102/103); Laif/Camera Press: R. Welham (80/81); Laif/Le Figaro Magazine: Prignet (69, 86/87); Laif/REA: F. Maravaux (10); S. Lier (135); mauritius images: G. Schade (85, 113); mauritius images/age fotostock: P. Schickert (58); mauritius images/Alamy: H. Blossey (54), Y. Turkov (56/57), K. Zelazowski (98/99); mauritius images/Alamy/Alamy Stock Photos Imagebroker/Iain Sharp (82); mauritius images/Almy/AlexelA (51); mauritius images/Alamy/Panther Medi GmbH (72/73); mauritius images/Dosphotos/Axiom Photographic (21); mauritius images/Hemis.fr: R. Mattes (6/7); mauritius images/Hemis.fr : P. Jacques (118/119); mauritius images/Imagebroker: M. Mainka (132/133), M. Weber (92), M. Wolf (47); mauritius images/Masterfile: R. I. Lloyd (11, 14/15, 100/101, 120/121, 122); mauritius images/robertharding: O. Wintzen (96/97); mauritius images/SagaPhoto: P. Forget (25); mauritius images/Westend61: M. Reuse (117)

All rights reserved. No part of this book may be reproduced, stored in a retrieval system or transmitted in any form or by any means (electronic, mechanical, photocopying, recording or otherwise) without prior written permission from the publisher.

1st Edition – 2024
Worldwide Distribution: Heartwood Publishing Ltd, Bath, United Kingdom
www.heartwoodpublishing.co.uk

Author: Sara Lier
Editor: Nikolai Michaelis
Picture editor: Gabriele Forst
Cartography: © 2023 KOMPASS-Karten GmbH, A-6020 Innsbruck; MAIRDUMONT, D-73751 Ostfildern (pp. 06–107, 109, 112, 115, 118, back cover, folding map); © 2023 KOMPASS-Karten GmbH, A-6020 Innsbruck; DuMont Reiseverlag, D-73751 Ostfildern (pp. 104, 108, 112, inset folding map); 2023 KOMPASS-Karten GmbH, kompass.de using
© OpenStreetMap Contributors, osm.org/copyright (pp. 28–29, 32, 39, 44, 49, 53, 62–63, 76–77, 88–89)
Cover design and pull-out map cover design: bilekjaeger_Kreativagentur with Zukunftswerkstatt, Stuttgart
Page design: Langenstein Communication GmbH, Ludwigsburg

Heartwood Publishing credits:
Translated from the German by Madeleine Oldham
Editors: Felicity Laughton, Kate Michell, Rosamund Sales, Sophie Blacksell Jones
Prepress: Summerlane Books, Bath
Printed in India

MARCO POLO AUTHOR
SARA LIER

Originally from Germany, geographer Sara Lier has been living in Portugal for over a decade now. Her friends in Porto don't understand why she adopted Lisbon as her home, and she does love Porto's northern charms at least as much as those of its rival further south. Luckily, as a travel writer and study abroad guide, she is regularly able to enjoy the rugged beauty of Porto.

DOS & DON'TS

HOW TO AVOID SLIP-UPS & BLUNDERS

DON'T WEAR THE WRONG STRIP
Football can be a serious business here, especially when it comes to the rivalry between FC Porto and SLB (Benfica Lisbon). Best not walk around Porto wearing the red shirt of the capital city club.

DO SPEAK PORTUGUESE
Yes, most Portuguese people understand Spanish. But their history dictates they want to be viewed as Portuguese and not Spanish. So for thank you, it's best to stick to *obrigado* (for men) or *obrigada* (for women).

DON'T JUMP THE QUEUE
If you find yourself waiting for the bus, you'll probably see everyone standing in line. Even if there's no discernible queue, the Portuguese know exactly who was there first and in which order you're getting on the bus! So pay attention and never just push your way to the front.

DON'T PAY OVER THE ODDS FOR TOO MUCH FISH
In restaurants, fresh fish and seafood are usually priced by the kilo ... which can lead to gasps of shock when you come to pay the bill. So get fish and shellfish weighed in advance to avoid any nasty surprises.

DON'T GET STUCK IN TRAFFIC
If you have rented a car, whatever you do, stay away from the Old Town! It was built long before cars were an issue and a narrow alley can get very narrow indeed! If a brave local resident has parked up somewhere, you may well find it too late to turn around ...